Congressional
Research
Service

Defense: FY2013 Authorization and Appropriations

Pat Towell
Specialist in U.S. Defense Policy and Budget

Daniel H. Else
Specialist in National Defense

September 5, 2012

Congressional Research Service

7-5700

www.crs.gov

R42607

CRS Report for Congress

Prepared for Members and Committees of Congress

Summary

President Obama's $613.9 billion FY2013 budget request for the Department of Defense (DOD) is $31.8 billion less than was appropriated for the agency in FY2012. The end of U.S. combat in Iraq and the declining tempo of operations in Afghanistan account for the bulk of the overall reduction: The budget request for Overseas Contingency Operations (OCO)—DOD activities in those two countries—is $88.5 billion, which is $26.6 billion less than was provided for those operations in FY2012.

However, the Administration's $525.4 billion request for DOD's so-called "base budget"—funds for all DOD activities other than OCO—is $5.2 billion less than was provided for FY2012 and $45.3 billion less than the FY2013 base budget the Administration had projected a year earlier, in February of 2011. The proposed reduction in the base budget—and planned reductions of more than $50 billion per year through FY2021, compared with the FY2011 projection—reflects the Administration's effort to reduce federal spending as required by the Budget Control Act (BCA) of 2011, enacted on August 2, 2011 (P.L. 112-25). All told, the Obama Administration's current projection would reduce DOD budgets by $486.9 billion over a 10-year period (FY2012-FY2021), compared with its February 2011 plan. (See "**FY2013 Defense Budget Overview**.")

According to the Administration, the FY2013 DOD budget request is consistent with the initial spending caps set by the BCA. However, both H.R. 4310, the version of the FY2013 National Defense Authorization passed by the House on May 18, 2012, and H.R. 5856, the companion DOD appropriations bill for FY2013, reported by the House Appropriations Committee on May 25, 2012, would exceed the Administration request—by $3.7 billion in the case of the authorization bill and by $3.1 billion in the case of the appropriation bill.

On the other hand, S. 3254, the version of the National Defense Authorization Act (NDAA) reported June 4, 2012, by the Senate Armed Services Committee, and the version of the DOD appropriations bill (H.R. 5856) reported by the Senate Appropriations Committee on August 2, 2012, would keep FY2013 DOD funding within the initial BCA caps.

The House and Senate versions of the authorization bill would add several billion dollars and overturn several cost-cutting initiatives incorporated in the Administration's budget, including proposed reductions in the Air Force Reserve and the Air National Guard. However, the House version would go further in rejecting the proposed savings. Similarly, while both versions of the authorization bill would add funding for programs Congress historically has favored (such as missile defense and equipment for reserve and National Guard forces), the Senate bill is more generous in this regard. (See "**NDAA: The Broad Outlines**.")

In general terms, the House-passed and Senate committee-reported versions of the DOD appropriations bill (H.R. 5856) parallel the House and Senate versions of the NDAA, respectively. (See "**DOD Appropriations Overview**.")

Contents

Figures

Tables

Appendixes

Contacts

Status of Legislation

Table 1. FY2013 National Defense Authorization Act (H.R. 4310; S. 3254)

Subcommittee Markups		House Report	House Passage	Senate Report	Senate Passage	Conf. Report	Conference Report Approval		Public Law
House	Senate						House	Senate	
4/26-27/2012	5/22-23/2012	5/9/2012 H.Rept. 112-479	5/18/2012 299-120	6/4/2012 S.Rept. 112-173					

Table 2. FY2013 DOD Appropriations Act (H.R. 5856)

Subcommittee Markup		House Report	House Passage	Senate Report	Senate Passage	Conf. Report	Conference Report Approval		Public Law
House	Senate						House	Senate	
5/8/2012	7/31/2012	5/25/2012 H.Rept. 112-493	7/19/2012 326-90	8/2/1012 S.Rept. 112-196					

FY2013 Defense Budget Overview

The Obama Administration's FY2013 budget request, submitted to Congress on February 13, 2012, includes $647.4 billion for the so-called "national defense" function (budget function 050). This includes funding for global operations of the Department of Defense (DOD), defense-related nuclear programs conducted by the Department of Energy, and other defense-related activities.

For discretionary DOD budget authority, the request includes $613.9 billion, of which $525.4 billion is for "base" defense budget costs—that is, day-to-day operations other than war costs— and the remaining $88.5 billion is for "Overseas Contingency Operations" (OCO)—that is, military operations in Afghanistan and elsewhere. The function 050 total also includes $18.0 billion for Department of Energy defense-related programs (dealing with nuclear weapons and warship powerplants), $4.7 billion for FBI national security programs, and $2.4 billion for a number of smaller accounts, including the selective service and civil defense (**Table 3**).

Excluding OCO funds, the Administration's FY2013 request for the national defense function totals $550.6 billion. The Congressional Budget Office (CBO) estimates the cost of Administration's program to be slightly higher: $552 billion.

Table 3. FY2013 National Defense Budget Function (050): Administration Request

budget authority in billions of dollars; numbers may not add due to rounding

			discretionary	mandatory	TOTAL
Department of Defense	Base Budget	TRICARE-for-Life accrual payment	6.68		
		Concurrent Receipt accrual payment		6.85	
		Other DOD Base Budget (incl. offsetting receipts)	518.77	-0.69	531.61
	Overseas Contingency Operations (OCO)		88.48		88.48
	DOD total		613.93	6.16	620.09
Defense-related Agencies	Energy Department	Occupational illness compensation and other		1.17	19.15
		Other Base Budget	17.98		
	FBI defense-related		4.75		4.75
	CIA Retirement Fund			0.51	0.51
	Other		2.42	0.06	2.48
National Defense Total			639.08	7.90	646.97
National Defense (excluding OCO)			550.60	6.16	556.76

Source: H.Rept. 112-479, House Armed Services Committee, Report on H.R. 4310, National Defense Authorization Act for FY2013, pp. 21-23.

Note: In the President's budget, these funds comprise Budget Function 050 (National Defense). In the budget resolution adopted March 29 by the House, the funds for Overseas Contingency Operations were incorporated into a separate function, designated Function 970.

If accepted by Congress, the Administration's DOD budget would mark the third consecutive annual decrease in total DOD funding (including OCO) since FY2010. Most of that decline reflects the decrease in OCO spending for operations in Iraq and Afghanistan.

However, while the decline in war costs accounts for most of the reduction in DOD budgets since FY2010, the President's FY2013 request would reduce the base budget (in current dollars) for the first time since 1996. The base budget request is $5.2 billion less than was appropriated for the base budget in FY2012 and $45.3 billion less than the FY2013 request the Administration had projected in February 2011 (**Figure 1**).

Figure 1. DOD Discretionary Budget Authority, FY2007-FY2013

amounts in billions of dollars

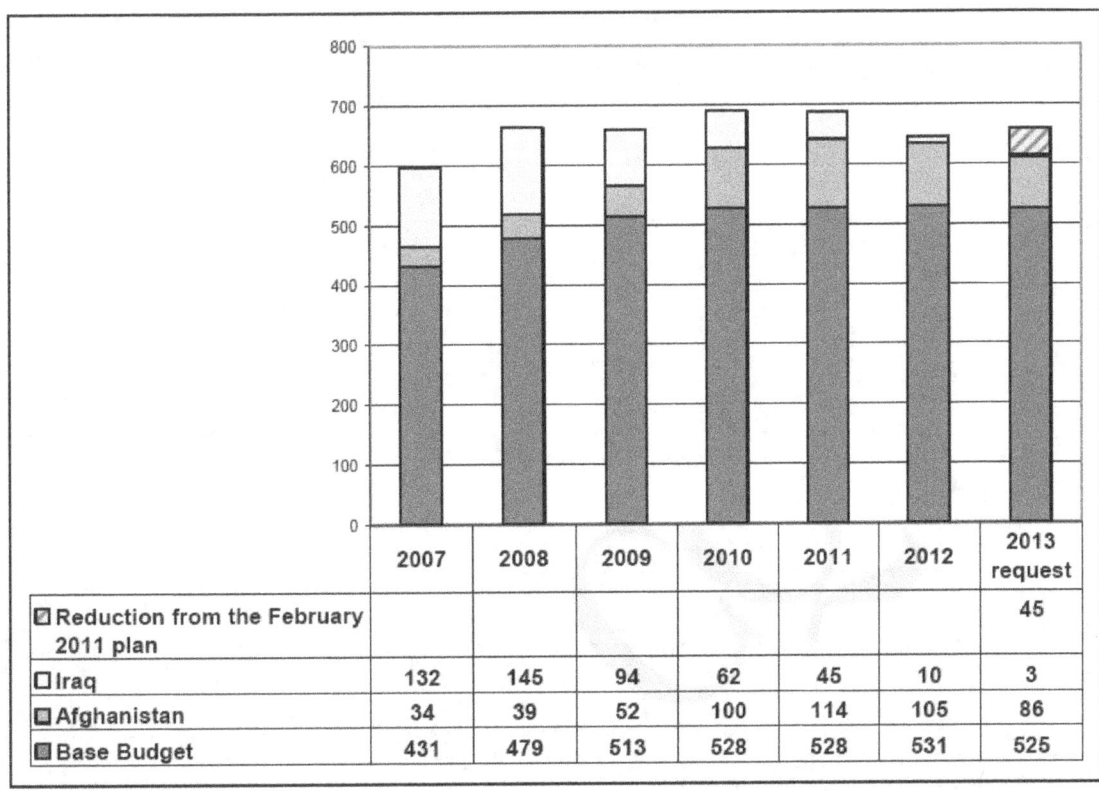

	2007	2008	2009	2010	2011	2012	2013 request
▨ Reduction from the February 2011 plan							45
▢ Iraq	132	145	94	62	45	10	3
▨ Afghanistan	34	39	52	100	114	105	86
▨ Base Budget	431	479	513	528	528	531	525

Source: DOD Comptroller, FY2013 Budget Request Overview, Figures 1-2 and 6-2, accessed at http://comptroller.defense.gov/defbudget/fy2013/FY2013_Budget_Request_Overview_Book.pdf.

That reduction from the previously planned FY2013 request—and additional planned reductions of more than $50 billion per year compared to DOD's February 2011 budget projections through FY2021—reflects the Administration's plan to reduce federal spending as required by the Budget Control Act (BCA) of 2011, enacted on August 2, 2011 (P.L. 112-25). Compared with the long-range spending plan published by DOD in February 2011, the February 2012 plan would reduce DOD base budgets by $259.4 billion from FY2012 through FY2017 (**Figure 2**). For the 10-year period covered by the BCA (FY2012-FY2021), the Administration's revised spending plan would reduce DOD budgets by a total of $486.9 billion.

**Figure 2. Obama Administration DOD Budget Projections:
February 2011 and February 2012**

amounts in billions of dollars

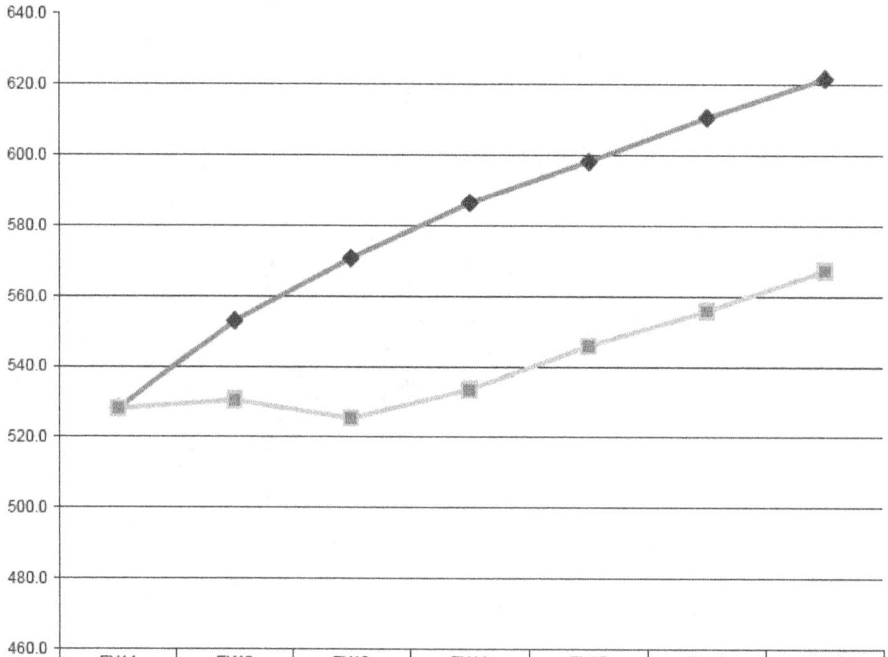

	FY11	FY12	FY13	FY14	FY15	FY16	FY17
DOD February 2011 Plan	528.2	553.0	570.7	586.4	598.2	610.6	621.6
DOD February 2012 Plan	528.2	530.6	525.4	533.6	545.9	555.9	567.3

Source: DOD Comptroller, Budget Briefing, FY2012 Budget Request (slide 4) accessed at
http://comptroller.defense.gov/defbudget/fy2013/FY2013_Budget_Request.pdf.

Further reductions in DOD base budgets over the next 10 years may be in store as a restul of the
BCA. In addition to the $900 billion worth of deficit reduction in FY2012-FY2021 (counting
both defense and non-defense spending) that results from the BCA, the act also requires
additional deficit reduction measures totaling $1.2 trillion through FY2021 (which would result in
a total deficit reduction through FY2021 of $2.1 trillion).

In FY2013, the BCA requires an across the board cut in budget authority (or "sequester") that
would be levied against almost all discretionary spending. For the National Defense budget
function (of which the DOD budget comprises more than 95 percent), some $59 billion—about
10 percent—would be cut from the Administration's budget request, with equal percentages cut
from each program, project and activity. In subsequent years, the BCA sets lowered spending
caps to achieve the required savings. Each year, to the extent that Congress appropriates more
than the caps allow, the Administration would sequester funds through across-the-board cuts to
ensure that the required savings are achieved. If the sequestration process and the lowered
spending caps remain law, the Administration's February 2012 projection for defense budgets
over the next 10 years would be cut by an additional $515 billion—about 9 percent.

Long-Term Budget Issues

For additional analysis of the potential impact on DOD of potential further budget reductions as part of the deficit reduction measures mandated by the Budget Control Act of 2011 (P.L. 112-25), see CRS Report R42489, *FY2013 Defense Budget Request: Overview and Context*, by Stephen Daggett and Pat Towell.

Base Budget Highlights

The Obama Administration presented its FY2013 DOD budget plan as an effort to both address the long-term spending limits set by the BCA and as an opportunity to refocus U.S. defense planning arising from the winding down of large-scale deployments of U.S. troops in Iraq and Afghanistan. The Administration preceded the announcement of its FY2013 budget request with the publication on January 5, 2012, of new "strategic guidance," which, it said, took account of both the new budgetary and strategic environments.[1]

New Strategic Guidance

The new strategic guidance postulates that active-duty ground forces no longer will be sized to conduct large-scale, prolonged stability operations such as those in Iraq and Afghanistan, which required an Army and Marine Corps capable of maintaining a constantly rotating overseas deployment of upwards of 100,000 troops.

Under this new approach, U.S. forces will be shaped and sized to conduct a campaign to defeat a major aggression—a combined arms campaign involving air, sea, and land forces and including a large-scale ground operation—and, simultaneously, another campaign intended to block an attack in some other area by a second adversary.[2]

The new strategic guidance also calls for DOD to put a higher priority on deploying U.S. forces to the Pacific and around Asia while scaling back deployments in Europe. For example, the Administration plans to withdraw and disband two of the four Army brigade combat teams currently stationed in Germany while maintaining a rotating force of up to 2,500 Marines in northern Australia. It also plans to station littoral combat ships in Singapore and smaller patrol craft in Bahrain. Because of the distances from land bases to which U.S. forces have access, operations in the Asia-Pacific region would rely heavily on air and naval forces. Accordingly, many observers expect a shift of DOD resources toward naval and air forces at the expense of ground formations.

Some question the Administration's claim of a "pivot" toward Asia, citing its plan to retire some older, long-range cargo planes and to cut a total of $13.1 billion from projected shipbuilding budgets for FY2013-FY2017. But the Administration cites its decisions to retain in service 11

---

[1] DOD, Sustaining U.S. Global Leadership: Priorities for 21st Century Defense, January 2012, accessed at http://www.defense.gov/news/Defense_Strategic_Guidance.pdf.

[2] Ibid., p. 4.

---

aircraft carriers and to add other ships to its shipbuilding plan as proof of its refocused commitment on the Pacific region, where long operational distances are the rule.

New Strategic Guidance and the 'Pivot to the Pacific'

For further analysis of the Obama Administration's new Strategic Guidance, issued in January 2012, see CRS Report R42146, *In Brief: Assessing DOD's New Strategic Guidance*, by Catherine Dale and Pat Towell. For additional analysis of the Administration's increased emphasis on Asia and the Pacific region as the focus of U.S. military and diplomatic attention, see CRS Report R42448, *Pivot to the Pacific? The Obama Administration's "Rebalancing" Toward Asia*, coordinated by Mark E. Manyin.

Force Structure, Readiness

Pursuant to the Administration's new strategic guidance, DOD plans to eliminate or retire several major combat units and weapons systems by FY2017. Among these are

- At least 8 of the Army's 45 active-duty brigade combat teams;
- Six of the Marine Corps' 41 battalion landing teams;
- Seven cruisers from, among the Navy's current fleet of 101 surface warships;
- Two of the Navy's 30 amphibious landing ships;
- Six of the 61 fighter and ground-attack squadrons in the Air Force, Air Force Reserve, and Air National Guard;
- 27 early-model C-5A cargo planes out of a total fleet of 302 long-range, wide-body C-5 and C-17 cargo jets;
- The entire fleet of C-27 mid-sized cargo planes, currently operated by the Air Force but desired by the Army to deliver supplies to troops in forward positions; and
- The entire fleet of "Block 30" Global Hawk surveillance drones, which DOD officials said had proven to be more expensive than the U-2 aircraft they had been slated to replace.

On the other hand, the Administration says its plan would maintain the remaining force at a high level of readiness. Compared with the February 2011 plan, the Operation and Maintenance request for FY2013 was reduced by 3%, one-fifth as large as the 15% reduction imposed on the Procurement accounts. (**Table 4**)

Table 4. FY2013 DOD Discretionary Budget Authority: February 2011 Projection and February 2012 Request

(amounts in billons of current year dollars)

Appropriations Title	Projected FY2013 Request Feb. 2011	Actual FY2013 Request Feb. 2012	Difference ($)	Difference (%)
Base Budget				
Military Personnel	141.82	135.11	-6.71	-4.7%
Operation and Maintenance	197.21	208.76	+11.55	+5.9%

Appropriations Title	Projected FY2013 Request Feb. 2011	Actual FY2013 Request Feb. 2012	Difference ($)	Difference (%)
Procurement	104.53	98.82	-5.70	-5.5%
RDT&E	71.38	69.41	-1.97	-2.8%
Military Construction	11.37	9.57	-1.79	-1.6%
Family Housing	1.68	1.65	-0.03	-1.9%
Revolving and Management Funds	2.64	2.12	-0.52	-19.7%
subtotal: Base Budget	530.62	525.45	-5.18	-1.0%
subtotal: Overseas Contingency Operations (OCO)	115.08	88.48	-26.60	-23.1%
TOTAL	645.71	613.93	-31.78	-4.9%

Source: DOD Comptroller, FY2013 Budget Request Overview, Table 8-1, accessed at http://comptroller.defense.gov/defbudget/fy2013/FY2013_Budget_Request_Overview_Book.pdf

Notes: The "Military Personnel" amounts include accrual payments into the budget account that funds TRICARE-for-Life, which is the program that allows military retirees not yet eligible for Medicare to remain enrolled in DOD's TRICARE medical insurance program. TRICARE-for-Life funds are not provided by the annual defense appropriations but, rather, by permanent law according to calculations by DOD actuaries.

Military Personnel Issues

The Administration plans to reduce the size of the active-duty force—slated to be 1.42 million at the end of FY2012—by 21,600 personnel in FY2013 and by a total of 102,400 by the end of FY2017. Consistent with the new policy of avoiding prolonged, large-scale peacekeeping operations, most of that multi-year reduction—92,000 out of the 102,400—would come from the Army and Marine Corps. In effect, this plan would remove from the force the 92,000 personnel that were added to the Army and Marine Corps beginning in 2007 to sustain deployments to Iraq and Afghanistan. However, in 2017—when the proposed reductions would be complete—each of those two services still would be larger than it had been before the terrorist attacks of September 11, 2001 (**Table 5**).

Table 5. Active Military End Strength

	FY2001	FY2012	FY2013 proposed	FY2017 Proposed
Army	480,801	562,000	552,100	490,000
Navy	377,810	325,700	322,700	319,500
Marine Corps	172,934	202,100	197,300	182,100
Air Force	353,571	332,800	328,900	328,600
Total	**1,385,116**	**1,422,600**	**1,401,000**	**1,320,200**

Source: DOD Comptroller, FY2013 Budget Request Overview, Figures 4-2, accessed at http://comptroller.defense.gov/defbudget/fy2013/FY2013_Budget_Request_Overview_Book.pdf

Pay Raise

The FY2013 budget request includes a 1.7% increase in service members' "basic pay," an amount based on the Labor Department's Employment Cost Index (ECI), which is a survey-based estimate of the rate at which private-sector pay has increased. After providing an equal increase in basic pay for FY2014, the Administration plan would provide basic pay raises less than the anticipated ECI increase in the following three years: 0.5% below ECI for FY2015, 1.0% below for FY2016, and 1.5% below for FY2017.

The Administration maintains that budgetary limits require some reduction in the rate of increase of military compensation in order to avoid excessive cuts in either the size of the force or the pace of modernization. However, it promises that no service member would be subjected to either a pay freeze or a pay cut. Moreover, proposed reductions in the size of the annual military pay raise would not begin until FY2015, thus allowing service members and their families to plan for the change. Over the five-year period (FY2013-FY2017), the Administration projects that savings from its planned schedule of military compensation would total $16.5 billion.

According to DOD officials, although military compensation accounts for about one-third of DOD's budget, the savings that would result from the proposed changes in compensation would account for less than 10% of the total that the Administration's budget would slice from the February 2011 DOD budget projection for FY2012-FY2021 (**Table 4**).

TRICARE Pharmacy Fees

The Administration also proposes a variety of fee increases for the 9.65 million beneficiaries of TRICARE, DOD's medical insurance program for active-duty, reserve-component, and retired service members and their dependents and survivors. According to DOD, the overall cost of the Military Health Program, which totaled $19 billion in FY2001, has more than doubled to $48.7 billion in FY2013. The FY2013 request assumes $1.8 billion in savings as a result of the Administration's proposed fee increases, which are controversial and which Congress would have to approve in law.

Many of the proposed fees and fee increases would apply only to working-age retirees and would be "tiered" according to the retiree's current income. The package also includes pharmacy co-pays intended to provide an incentive for TRICARE beneficiaries to use generic drugs and mail-order pharmacy service. Future changes in some of the propose fees and in the "catastrophic cap" per family would be indexed to the National Health Expenditures (NHE) index, a measure of escalation in medical costs calculated by the federal agency that manages Medicare.

Modernization

Compared with the FY2013 budget that DOD projected in February of 2011, the actual FY2013 request for procurement and R&D accounts was 12.5% lower. Proportionally, that reduction is more than twice as large as the reduction in the combined accounts for military personnel and operation and maintenance (down 4.7%).

Measured in constant dollars, DOD's combined procurement and R&D budget in FY2010 was 60% higher than it had been in FY2001. Accordingly, some argue that DOD can afford to rein in its spending on acquisition while it lives off the capital stocks built up and modernized during the decade of budget increases that followed the terrorist attacks of 2001.[3]

But others contend that much of the procurement spending during that decade was for (1) items peculiarly relevant to the wars in Iraq and Afghanistan; (2) items needed to replace equipment destroyed in combat or worn out by the high tempo of operations in a region that is particularly stressful on machinery and electronics; or (3) modifications to existing planes, tanks, and ships. While modifications can improve the effectiveness of existing platforms, they cannot nullify in the long run the impact of age and design obsolescence.[4]

The Administration emphasizes that it is prioritizing among weapons programs in deciding where to make cuts in previously planned spending and that it is sustaining funding for high-priority programs, such as the development of a new, long-range bomber for which its plan budgets $292 million in FY2013 and more than $5 billion in FY2014-FY2017.

Compared with DOD's February 2011 plan for procurement and R&D funding, the program announced in February 2013 would save $24 billion in FY2013 and a total of $94 billion over the five-year period FY2013-FY2017. Procurement of some items would be terminated outright, before the originally planned total number was acquired (e.g., the Army's new 5-ton trucks—designated FMTV—terminated for a total savings of $2.2 billion over five years, and a new Air Force weather satellite, terminated for a total savings of $2.3 billion).

But DOD plans to achieve most of the savings in procurement from "restructuring" programs, that is, from slowing the timetable for moving from development into production or slowing the rate of production. The department justifies some of its proposed reductions on grounds of fact-of-life delays in specific programs. In other cases, it contends that it is an "acceptable risk" to forego (or delay) acquisition of a particular capability.

Overseas Contingency Operations Highlights

The Administration's $88.5 billion request for war costs (OCO) amounts to $26.6 billion less than Congress appropriated for war costs in FY2012. This reduction reflects:

- the cessation of U.S. combat operations in Iraq by the end of the first quarter of FY2012; and

- the reduction of the number of U.S. troops in Afghanistan, by the end of FY2012, to 68,000 personnel, thus ending the "surge" into that country of 33,000 additional U.S. troops announced by President Obama on December 1, 2009.

---

[3] See, for example, Stimson Center, "What We Bought: Defense Procurement from FY01 to FY10," by Russell Rumbaugh, October 2011.

[4] See, for example, American Enterprise Institute, "The Past Decade of Military Spending: What We Spent, What we Wasted, and What We Need," by Mackenzie Eaglen, January 24, 2012.

Figure 3. OCO Funding by Country

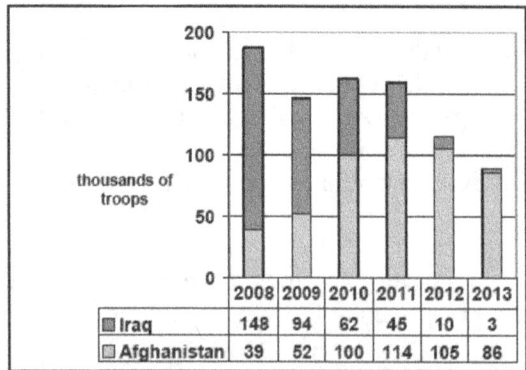

	2008	2009	2010	2011	2012	2013
Iraq	148	94	62	45	10	3
Afghanistan	39	52	100	114	105	86

Source: DOD Comptroller, FY2013 Budget Request Overview, Figure 6-2, accessed at http://comptroller.defense.gov/defbudget/fy2013/FY2 013_Buget_Request_Overview_Book.pdf.

Figure 4. U.S. Troop Level by Country

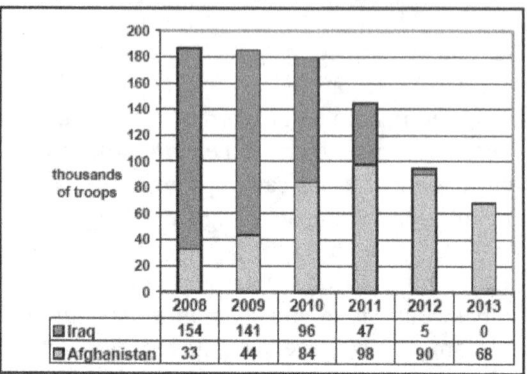

	2008	2009	2010	2011	2012	2013
Iraq	154	141	96	47	5	0
Afghanistan	33	44	84	98	90	68

Source: DOD Comptroller, FY2013 Budget Request Overview, Figure 6-2, accessed at http://comptroller.defense.gov/defbudget/fy2013/FY2 013_Buget_Request_Overview_Book.pdf.

The OCO budget request assumes that 68,000 U.S. troops will remain in Afghanistan through the end of FY2013, although President Obama has said that, after the number had been drawn down to 68,000 by the summer of 2012, it would continue to decline "at a steady pace." [5]

Bill-by-Bill Analysis

FY2013 National Defense Authorization Act

The House version of the FY2013 National Defense Authorization Act (NDAA), passed May 18 by a vote of 229-199, would authorize $3.7 billion more than the $631.6 billion President Obama requested for discretionary DOD spending and for defense-related nuclear energy programs conducted by the Department of Energy. The bill was thus consistent with the FY2013 budget resolution (H.Con.Res. 112, adopted by the House on March 29, 2012), but would exceed by $8 billion the revised defense budget cap established by the 2011 BCA. That revised cap would be the basis for a sequester in January 2013, unless the BCA is superseded by subsequent legislation.

The Senate Armed Services Committee reported its version of the FY2013 NDAA (S. 3254) on May 25. That bill would authorize $234 million less than the President's request (**Table 6**).

---

[5] President Barack Obama, Remarks by the President on the Way Forward in Afghanistan, Washington, DC, June 22, 2011, available at http://www.whitehouse.gov/the-press-office/2011/06/22/remarks-president-way-forward-afghanistan.

Table 6. FY2013 National Defense Authorization Act (H.R. 4310; S. 3254)

(amounts of discretionary budget authority in millions of dollars)

	FY2013 Administration Request	FY2013 House-passed H.R. 4310	FY2013 SASC-reported S. 3254	FY2013 Conference Report
Procurement	97,432	99,122	96,959	
Research and Development	69,408	70,387	69,286	
Operations and Maintenance	174,939	175,082	174,778	
Military Personnel	135,112	135,727	135,112	
Defense Health Program and Other Authorizations	37,228	37,458	37,739	
Military Construction and Family Housing	11,223	10,838	10,559	
Commission on the Structure of the Air Force			1,400	
Subtotal: DOD Base Budget	525,342	528,614	525,839	
Subtotal: Atomic Energy Defense Activities (Energy Dept.)	17,779	18,143	17,348	
TOTAL: FY2013 Base Budget	543,121	546,757	543,187	
Subtotal: Overseas Contingency Operations	88,482	88,482	88,182	
GRAND TOTAL: FY2013 NDAA	631,603	635,259	631,369	
National Defense Discretionary Funding not covered by this bill	7,474	7,474	7,474	
Total: FY2013 National Defense Discretionary Budget Authority implications of the bill	639,077	642,713	638,843	
FY2013 Mandatory National Defense Funding	7,891	7,891	7,891	
Grand Total FY2013 National Defense Budget Authority Implications of the bill	646,968	650,579	646,734	

Source: H.Rept. 112-479, House Armed Services Committee, Report on H.R. 4310, National Defense Authorization Act for FY2013, pp. 10-19; S.Rept. 112-173, Senate Armed Services Committee, Report on S. 3254, National Defense Authorization Act for FY2013, pp. 4-8.

Note: The amounts requested and authorized in the annual National Defense Authorization Act (NDAA) is less than the total National Defense Budget because defense-related activities conducted by agencies other than DOD and the Energy Department—for example, the FBI's counterintelligence activity—are not covered by the bill and because certain DOD activities do not require annual authorization.

NDAA: The Broad Outlines

Compared with annual defense authorization bills enacted in the previous decade, both H.R. 4310 as passed by the House and S. 3254 as reported by the Senate Armed Services Committee would make relatively few changes in the authorization levels proposed by the Administration for specific programs. This reflects the stringent bars against "earmarks" currently observed in both the House and the Senate.

A small number of factors summarized below account for most of the $3.9 billion difference between the total amounts that would be authorized by the two bills.

Proposed Administration Savings

H.R. 4310 would add to the request more than $4 billion to cover the cost of overturning some of the Administration's more high-profile efforts to reduce DOD spending. The Senate committee's bill would take similar action to reverse two of the initiatives—disbanding several squadrons of airplanes in the Air Force, Air Force Reserve, and Air National Guard; and deferring production of an attack submarine. However, the Senate panel's bill would support, wholly or in part, several of the Administration's other proposed DOD spending cuts:

Selected Administration proposals	H.R. 4310 House-passed	S. 3254 Committee-reported
Disband 7 Air Force and Air National Guard squadrons; Retire 303 aircraft.	Adds authorization for $1.1 billion and 7,816 personnel (active duty and reserve components) to retain the current force structure.	Freezes current force structure; prohibits retirement of aircraft; adds $1.4 billion to cover the cost of maintaining status quo; creates commission to recommend future force structure of Air Force (including reserve components).
Cancel planned procurements of Global Hawk Block 30 surveillance drones; Retire Global Hawk 30s in service.	Adds $260 million to continue Global Hawk Block 30 operations.	In effect, withdraws $544 million appropriated for Global Hawk Block 30 in prior years, directing that those funds be substituted for new budget authority to fund the FY2013 budget.
Retire four Aegis cruisers.	Adds $665 million to keep in service three of the four cruisers.	n/c
Increase various TRICARE fees, reducing the FY2013 budget requirement by $1.8 billion.	Adds $1.21 billion to replace funds the Administration had planned to obtain from fee changes which the House bill would not authorize; Allows some requested increases.	Adds $452 million to replace funds the Administration had planned to obtain from fee changes which the House bill would not authorize; Allows larger number of requested increases.
Slow design of new ballistic missile sub, reducing FY2013 funding by more than half ($640 million) from earlier projection.	Adds $374 million to fund ship design at earlier projected level; No addition to restore funds cut from nuclear reactor design.	n/c
Buy components to support purchase of one Virginia-class submarine in FY2014 rather than two, reducing FY2013 funding by more than 40% ($667 million).	Adds $778 million to allow funding two subs in FY2014.	Adds $778 million to allow funding two subs in FY2014.

Selected Administration proposals	H.R. 4310 House-passed	S. 3254 Committee-reported
Slow development of Army's Ground Combat Vehicle reducing FY2013 funding by two-thirds ($1.3 billion) from earlier projection.	n/c	n/c

Notes: The notation "n/c" ["no change"] signifies that no provision of the bill would block or alter the proposed policy.

Other Increased Weapons Spending

Senate Armed Services Committee's version of the FY2013 NDAA also was more restrained than H.R. 4310 in funding certain programs for which Congress typically adds to the annual budget request:

Selected Administration proposals	H.R. 4310 House-passed	S. 3254 Committee-reported
Request $903 million to continue upgrading Ballistic Missile Defense that has interceptor missiles based in Alaska and California.	Adds $357 million to deploy additional interceptor missiles in Alaska and $103 million to begin work on an East Coast site for additional interceptors.	n/c
Request $100 million to continue development of three Israeli missile defense systems.	Adds $168 million for those three Israeli systems and an additional $680 million for the Israeli "Iron Dome" system designed to intercept short-range rockets and artillery shells.	Adds $100 million for the three Israeli systems and an additional $210 million for "Iron Dome."
Phase out upgrades to Abrams tanks and Bradley troop carriers preparatory to shutting down those production lines from 2014 until 2017, when new upgrade programs would begin.	Adds $320 million to continue Abrams and Bradley upgrades.	Adds $91 million to continue Abrams upgrades.
Request no funding for the National Guard and Reserve Equipment account (NGREA)	Adds $500 million for NGREA.	n/c

Notes: The notation "n/c" ["no change"] signifies that no provision of the bill would block or alter the proposed policy.

Funding Offsets

As is customary in annual NDAAs, both the House-passed H.R. 4310 and the Senate committee's S. 3254 would offset some or all of their proposed additions to the budget request with some relatively large proposed reductions within certain programs. Moreover—as usual—the House and Senate Armed Services Committees that drafted the two bills said that some of their proposed reductions would have no adverse impact on DOD. For example, each bill would reduce the total amount authorized by upwards of $1.5 billion on the grounds that funds appropriated in prior years but not spent could be used in lieu of the same amount of new budget authority to cover part of the FY2013 budget:

Issue	H.R. 4310 House-passed	S. 3254 Committee-reported
Amounts appropriated in prior budgets, now deemed unnecessary for their original purpose, are redirected to fund the FY2013 program (thus reducing the requirement for new budget authority by the same amount).	Cuts a total of $1.61 billion from military personnel, O&M and Defense Health Program requests on the grounds that, historically, those accounts have "underspent" their appropriations, thus leaving "unobligated balances" in the accounts at the end of the fiscal year.	Cuts a total of $1.50 billion from procurement, R&D, O&M and military construction requests on grounds that an equal amount, appropriated in prior budgets, can be substituted for new budget authority. This includes $544.4 million in prior year funding for the Global Hawk Block 30, which the Administration proposes cancelling.
Missile Defense Programs	Cuts the entire $400.9 million requested for MEADS missile defense system, a joint project of the U.S., German, and Italian governments.	Cuts the entire $400.9 million requested for MEADS missile defense system, a joint project of the U.S., German and Italian governments. Also cuts $247.4 million (of $297.4 million requested) for Precision Tracking Space System (PTSS) missile tracking program.
Aid to Afghanistan and to other governments collaborating with U.S. policy in Afghanistan.	Cuts a total of $1.00 billion from the request, including $650.0 million from Coalition Support Funds and $200.0 million from Commanders Emergency Response Program (CERP).	Cuts a total of $250 million from the request, including $200.0 million from Commanders Emergency Response Program (CERP).
$911.0 million request to decommission the nuclear-powered carrier USS *Enterprise*.	Cuts $470.0 million that would not be needed until FY2014, directing the Navy to fund the project on a year-by-year basis.	n/c
$463.0 million request for Energy Department contribution to fund for environmental cleanup at U.S. uranium enrichment facilities.	n/c	Cuts the entire amount on grounds that payments must be authorized by legislation outside jurisdiction of Armed Services Committee.

Notes: The notation "n/c" ["no change"] signifies that no provision of the bill would block or alter the proposed policy.

Military Personnel Issues

H.R. 4310 as passed by the House and S. 3254 as reported by the Senate committee would authorize a 1.7% military pay raise, as requested. Both also would reject Administration proposals to reduce the size of the Air Force and associated reserve components.

In their respective reports on the two bills, the Armed Services Committees of the House and Senate each express concern that the Administration's plan to reduce the Army and Marine Corps by a total of 92,000 by the end of FY2017 may cut too deep. However, both bills would authorize the Administration's proposed reductions in the number of active-duty personnel for the Army, Navy, and Marine Corps in FY2013 (**Table 7**).

**Table 7. Current and Proposed FY2013 End-Strength
for Active and Reserve Component Forces**

Service	FY2012 Authorized	FY2013 Request	H.R. 4310 passed by the House		S. 3254 reported by SASC	
			number authorized	change from request	number authorized	change from request
ACTIVE FORCES						
Army	562,000	552,100	552,100	0	552,100	0
Navy	325,700	322,700	322,700	0	322,700	0
Marine Corps	202,100	197,300	197,300	0	197,300	0
Air Force	332,800	328,900	329,597	+697	330,383	+1,483
TOTAL Active Forces	1,422,600	1,401,000	1,401,697	+697	1,401,560	+1,483
SELECTED RESERVE						
Army National Guard	358,200	358,200	358,200	0	358,200	0
Army Reserve	205,000	205,000	205,000	0	205,000	0
Navy Reserve	66,200	66,200	66,200	0	66,200	0
Marine Corps Reserve	39,600	39,600	39,600	0	39,600	0
Air National Guard	106,700	101,600	105,005	+4,405	106,435	+4,835
Air Force Reserve	71,400	70,500	72,428	+1,928	72,428	+1,928
TOTAL Selected Reserve	847,100	837,400	843,733	+6,333	844,163	+6,763

Note: The "Selected Reserve" are those reservists enrolled in units that assemble for drill periods a certain number of times annually, including one period of two weeks duration. Service members enrolled in other reserve categories do not participate in regular drills.

Proposed Reductions in Personnel and Force Structure

Air Force Cuts

Both versions of the bill contain provisions that would block the Administration's proposal to disband several Air Force units and retire more than 300 aircraft. In testimony before the Senate Defense Appropriations Subcommittee on March 14, 2012, Air Force Secretary Michael Donley said he would defer the proposed changes until Congress completes action on the FY2013 defense funding bills. In a June 22, 2012, letter to Senate Defense Subcommittee Chairman Daniel K. Inouye, Defense Secretary Panetta went further, saying he would defer any changes to the force structure of the Air Force—including some that had been authorized and funded in prior budgets—until Congress completes work on the FY2013 budget.

The House bill would authorize 7,030 personnel more than requested for the Air Force and its associated reserve components in order to staff units that had been slated for disbanding. H.R. 4310 would add to the request $699.2 million to continue operating those units, plus $400.4

million to continue purchasing C-27 cargo planes and RQ-4 Block 30 Global Hawk reconnaissance drones. The Administration had proposed mothballing the C-27s and Block 30 Global Hawks already in hand and terminating plans to buy more of each.[6]

The Senate committee bill would authorize 8,246 more personnel than had been requested for the Air Force and associated reserve components. S. 3254 also includes provisions that would add to the budget request a total of $1.40 billion to maintain the status quo pending recommendations by a National Commission on the Structure of the Air Force that the bill would establish (Sections 1701-1709). Those recommendations would be due by March 31, 2013.

However, the Senate committee bill would not challenge the Administration's proposal to dispose of the C-27s and Global Hawk Block 30s. In fact, it would—in effect—rescind $544 million appropriated for Global Hawk in prior years, using those funds instead to cover some of the cost of the FY2013 budget.

Ship Retirements

The House bill would bar the Navy from retiring three of the four Aegis cruisers the service wants to lay up as a cost-saving measure. However, H.R. 4310 would approve a reduction in Navy end-strength from 325,700 to 322,700, as requested. The Armed Services Committee said the Navy could man the three ships even after absorbing that reduction. The bill would allow the Navy to retire, as requested, the fourth cruiser, the USS *Port Royal*, although that ship—commissioned in 1994—is the newest of the Aegis cruisers and one of the few that has been modified to shoot down ballistic missiles. The ship sustained structural damage when it ran aground off Honolulu in 2009.

S. 3254 would allow the proposed cruiser retirements to proceed.

Army and Marine Corps Drawdown

The Armed Services Committees of both the House and Senate, in their reports on their respective versions of the defense authorization act, expressed concern over the Administration's plan to cut a total of 92,000 active-duty personnel from the Army and Marine Corps by the end of FY2017. Although both bills would authorize the portion of that long-term reduction that the Administration has proposed for FY2013 (approving cuts of 9,900 from the Army and 4,800 from the Marine Corps), the two committees warned that the reduction could undermine morale by reducing "dwell-time"—that is, the period during which soldiers and Marines are stationed at their home bases between overseas deployments.

H.R. 4310 includes a provision (Section 403) that would limit the number of personnel that could be cut in any one year from 2014 through 2017 to 15,000 from the Army and 5,000 from the Marine Corps. In its Statement of Administration Policy (SAP) on the bill, the Office of Management and Budget (OMB) said this provision would slow its planned drawdown in ground

---

[6] The Administration's proposal to abandon the Block 30 version of the Global Hawk has no effect on other versions of the Global Hawk long-range, unmanned aircraft used by DOD.

forces, thus increasing military personnel and health care costs by more than $500 million in 2014 and by a total of $1.9 billion through 2019.[7]

S. 3254 includes no such provision, but in its report to accompany the bill, the Senate Armed Services Committee directed DOD to include with each of its annual budget requests for FY2014-FY2017 two items relevant to this issue:

- A prediction of the ratio of "dwell time" to deployment time for active and reserve component personnel that would result from the personnel reductions proposed in that budget; and

- An assessment of whether the proposed reductions could be reversed within one year, if unforeseen contingencies led to the deployment of more forces than the budget request had assumed.

TRICARE

Neither the House-passed H.R. 4310 nor the Senate committee-reported S. 3254 would authorize most of the Administration's proposed new fees and fee increases for TRICARE beneficiaries and for retirees who benefit from the so-called TRICARE-for-Life program. Specifically, neither bill would authorize proposals to

- raise TRICARE-for-Life premiums for military retirees using a three-tier model linking the size of each beneficiary's increase to the amount of his or her military retired pay;

- link increases in TRICARE's so-called "catastrophic cap"—the maximum amount a family would have to pay in a single year—to increases in the federal government's National Health Expenditure index; and

- increase the annual enrollment fees for the TRICARE Prime plan and introduce enrollment fees for the other TRICARE plans, including TRICARE-for-Life.

The House bill (Section 718) would allow increases in the TRICARE co-pays for brand and non-formulary drugs, but at a lower rate than current law would allow. This section of the bill further provides that, beginning in 2014, pharmacy co-payments would be indexed to the annual retiree cost-of-living adjustment. The bill also directs the Secretary of Defense to conduct a pilot program that would use the national mail-order pharmacy program to refill prescription maintenance medications for each TRICARE-for-Life beneficiary (Section 717). All told, H.R. 4310 would add $1.21 billion to the amount requested in the budget to compensate for savings the Administration had anticipated would result from the proposed TRICARE changes the House bill would not make.

S. 3254 would allow the proposed increase in TRICARE pharmacy co-pays at the rate allowed by current law. It also would authorize $452 million more than was requested for DOD's health care

---

[7] Office of Management and Budget, "Statement of Administration Policy: H.R. 4310—National Defense Authorization Act for FY2013," accessed at http://www.whitehouse.gov/sites/default/files/omb/legislative/sap/112/saphr4310r_20120515.pdf.

program to compensate for savings projected to have resulted from TRICARE changes the bill would not authorize.

Abortion

The Senate committee-reported bill includes a provision (Section 711) that would authorize the use of DOD funds to provide abortions in the case of pregnancies resulting from rape or incest.

Same-Sex Marriage

The House bill includes a provision (Section 537) that would prohibit the use of DOD facilities for any marriage or "marriage-like" ceremony unless the ceremony involves the union of one man and one woman. The bill also includes a provision (Section 536) that would prohibit any military chaplain from being required to perform any duty or religious ceremony contrary to the chaplain's conscience or religious beliefs. The provision also would bar any adverse personnel action against a chaplain on the basis of his refusal to comply with any order prohibited by the Section.

Women in Combat Roles

In a February 2012 report mandated by Section 535 of the Ike Skelton National Defense Authorization Act for FY2011,[8] DOD announced its intention to relax several policies that have restricted the assignment of women to ground combat units and their associated support units. One of those announced changes was the development of "gender-neutral physical standards for occupational specialties closed [to women] due to physical requirements." H.R. 4310 includes a provision (Section 526) that would require DOD to report to Congress on the feasibility of developing such standards.

The House Armed Services Committee noted, in its report on H.R. 4310, that counterinsurgency operations in Iraq and Afghanistan "place female service members in direct combat action with the enemy." Noting that some women who had been deployed in that theater were critical of the body armor currently issued to U.S. troops (which was designed for male body morphology), the committee directed the Secretary of the Army to assess the need for body armor tailored to female body types.

The Senate Armed Services Committee, in its report on S. 3254, called the policy changes announced in DOD's February 2012 report "a small step in the right direction," but urged DOD to further relax current restrictions on the assignment of female service personnel, saying: "By limiting their use of the talents of female service members, the Department [of Defense] and the services are handicapping efforts to field the highest quality force possible."

The Senate committee directed the Secretary of Defense to report by February 1, 2013, on its implementation of the policy changes announced in the February report and to "make

---

[8] U.S. Department of Defense, Office of the Under Secretary of Defense (P&R), Report to Congress on the Reviews of Laws, Policies and Regulations Restricting the Service of Female Members in the U.S. Armed Forces, February, 2012.

recommendations for regulatory and statutory change that the Secretary considers appropriate to increase service opportunities for women in the armed forces."

Ground Combat Equipment

Congressional action on authorization of funding for selected ground force equipment is summarized in **Table A-3**. Following are highlights:

M-1 tanks, Bradley troop carriers, Hercules tank recovery vehicles

As part of DOD's strategic reorientation,[9] the Army plans to dissolve at least 8 of its 47 active-duty brigade combat teams (BCTs),[10] including at least 2 of its 15 so-called "heavy" BCTs—units equipped with dozens of M-1 Abrams tanks and Bradley armored troop carriers. The Army has not decided the final number of active BCTs it wants to retain; how many of that number will be heavy BCTs; or the number of tanks, Bradleys, and other armored combat vehicles in each heavy unit.

In its report on H.R. 4310, the House committee expressed concern that budget pressures might induce the Army to eliminate too many heavy BCTs (which cost more to equip and operate than other units). The panel also objected to DOD's plan to shut down, from 2013 through 2016, the production lines that upgrade M-1 tanks (in Lima, OH) and Bradleys (in York, PA). Under the Administration's plan, the two lines would re-open in 2017 to further modify tanks and Bradleys.

The House committee maintained that it was not clear either (1) that the planned temporary shut-downs would save very much or (2) that the network of suppliers needed to support planned future upgrades could be reconstituted after a three-year break. The panel also contended that there was a need for additional upgraded combat vehicles and that pending Army decisions might further increase the requirement. Accordingly, the House bill would increase above the budget request the amounts authorized for three of the Army's heavy combat vehicles, authorizing

- $255.4 million (an increase of $181.0 million) to convert older M-1As to the M-1A2 SEP configuration, with improvements to night-vision equipment and other components;

- $288.2 million (an increase of $140.0 million) to upgrade Bradleys; and

- $169.9 million to buy 51 Hercules tank recovery vehicles, designed to tow damaged tanks to safety (an increase of $62.0 million and 20 vehicles).

The House committee also urged the Army to accelerate a program to equip its 1980s-vintage Paladin mobile howitzers with a new chassis and a drive train adapted from the Bradley troop carrier.

---

[9] See "New Strategic Guidance," above.

[10] Brigade combat teams (BCTs), the Army's basic combat units, are manned by about 4,000 soldiers.

S. 3254, as reported by the Senate Armed Services Committee, would mirror the House bill's authorization of $255.4 million to convert older tanks to the M-1A2 SEP configuration. It would authorize the amount requested to upgrade Bradleys but would also authorize a total of $230.9 million for Hercules tank recovery vehicles.[11]

New Generation of Tactical Vehicles

H.R. 4310 and S. 3254 each would authorize the amounts requested to develop a new generation of Army vehicles:

- $639.9 million for the Ground Combat Vehicle, intended to replace the Bradley;

- $74.1 million for the Armored Multi-Purpose Vehicle (AMPV), intended to replace the Vietnam War-vintage M-113 troop carrier now used in various roles, including battlefield ambulance and supply hauler; and

- $116.8 million for the Joint Light Tactical Vehicle (JLTV), intended to succeed the jeep-like "Humvee" (HMMWV).

Naval Systems

Congressional action on authorization of funding for selected naval systems is summarized in **Table A-5**. Following are highlights.

Attack Submarines

As requested, H.R. 4310 and S. 3254 each would authorize $3.22 billion for two Virginia-class attack submarines. But both bills also would authorize $1.65 billion—$778.0 million more than requested—for long lead-time components to be used for an additional submarine to be procured in FY2014. The addition would allow the Navy to budget for two submarines in FY2014—as had been assumed in DOD's February 2011 budget projection—rather than one, as is assumed in the budget projection published in February 2012.

Each of the bills also includes a provision (Section 126 of H.R. 4310 and Section 124 of S. 3254) that would permit the use of a multi-year contract for procuring up to 10 Virginia-class attack submarines in FY2014-FY2018, and the use of incremental funding[12] in such a contract. The Navy had requested authority for a multi-year contract to buy nine submarines during that period. The service did not request authority to use incremental funding in the contract, but testified that

---

[11] The M88 Hercules is built from the chassis design of the M-1's predecessor, the M60 Patton tank. It is, in essence, a very large, heavy, and armored tow truck for tanks.

[12] In general, Congress requires that DOD budgets for weapons procurement adhere to a "full funding" policy, under which the entire procurement cost of a weapon or piece of equipment (except for certain "long lead-time" components) is appropriated in the year in which the item is procured. Under "incremental funding," a weapon's cost is divided into two or more annual portions, or increments, that reflect the need to make annual progress payments to the contractor as the weapon is built. Congress then approves each year's increment as part of its action on that year's budget. See CRS Report RL31404, *Defense Procurement: Full Funding Policy—Background, Issues, and Options for Congress*, by Ronald O'Rourke and Stephen Daggett.

it wanted to find a way, if possible, to buy a second Virginia-class boat in FY2014 (which would be the 10th boat in the multi-year contract), and that doing so would likely require the use of incremental funding.

DDG-51 Aegis Destroyers

The House-passed and Senate committee-reported bills each contain a provision relating to Aegis destroyers that parallels in some respects their respective provisions relating to attack subs. In both H.R. 4310 and S. 3254, Section 125 would permit the Navy to sign a multi-year contract to buy 10 Aegis destroyers in FY2013-FY2017. The Navy had requested authority for a multi-year contract to procure nine of the ships in that period, but indicated in testimony that it hoped that bids submitted for that contract might come in low enough to finance the procurement of a 10th ship.

As requested, both bills would authorize $3.05 billion for two destroyers in FY2013. But the House bill also would authorize $581.3 million—$115 million more than requested—for long lead-time components to be used for an additional (10th) ship.

Ballistic Missile Submarines

In February 2011, DOD projected a FY2013 budget request totaling $1.20 billion to continue developing a new class of 12 missile-launching submarines, designated SSBN(X). These ships are intended to replace the 14 Ohio-class subs built in the 1980s and 1990s, which are slated to begin retiring in 2027. The first of the new subs was slated to begin construction in FY2019. The Administration's FY2013 budget request, unveiled in February 2012, would provide less than half of the amount earlier projected for FY2013—$564.9 million—and would defer construction of the first of the new ships until FY2021.

FY2013 R&D funding related to SSBN(X) (amounts in millions of dollars)				
	Projected 2/2011	Requested 2/2012	H.R. 4310	S. 3254
Ship design	857.495	483.095	857.495	483.095
Nuclear reactor design	347.095	81.817	81.817	81.817
Total	1,204.590	564.913	939.312	564.913

In its report on H.R. 4310, the House committee objected that, under the new schedule, the number of missile subs in service would drop to 10 or 11 ships for a dozen years (2029-2041). It added to the bill a provision (Section 121) requiring the Navy to maintain a force of at least 12 ballistic missile submarines. The panel also added $374.4 million to the authorization requested to design the planned new sub, increasing that authorization to the level that had been projected in 2011. The House bill would authorize the amount requested to develop the new missile sub's nuclear powerplant.

S. 3254 would authorize the amounts requested for SSBN(X).

Action on Other Naval Programs

As requested, H.R. 4310 and S. 3254 each would authorize $608.2 million as the first of six annual funding increments[13] for procurement of the aircraft carrier USS *John F. Kennedy*, slated for delivery to the Navy in 2022. However, the House bill includes a provision (Section 123) that would allow the Navy to spend no more than half that amount in FY2013 until the Secretary of the Navy sends Congress a plan to implement detailed management and construction policies intended to keep the ship on budget.

In both H.R. 4310 and S. 3254, Section 122—requested by the Navy—would permit incremental funding for construction of this new carrier and its predecessor, the USS *Gerald R. Ford*, already under construction, to be spread over six years. Existing law permits five-year incremental funding for aircraft carriers.

The House bill would authorize a total of $665.1 million more than was requested to fund upgrades and continued operation of three of the four Aegis cruisers the Administration proposed retiring in FY2013. The largest single component of the addition is $170.0 million for five MH-60R Seahawk helicopters, which are carried by cruisers and many other warships.

The House bill also includes a provision (Section 1021) repealing Section 1012 of the FY2008 National Defense Authorization Act (P.L. 110-181), which required all major combatant vessels to be designed with nuclear power systems.

Aircraft and Long-Range Strike Systems

Congressional action on authorization of funding for selected aircraft and long-range strike programs is summarized in **Table A-10**. Following are some highlights.

Long-Range Bombers, Strike Weapons

As requested, each bill would authorize $291.7 million to continue developing a new, long-range bomber the Air Force wants to begin procuring in the 2020s. The House-passed H.R. 4310 includes a provision (Section 211) requiring that the airplane be equipped to carry nuclear weapons. The House rejected by a vote of 112-308 an amendment to delay the program by 10 years and eliminate the authorization for FY2013 funds (see H.Amdt. 1108 in **Table 8**).

Both the House-passed and Senate committee-reported bills also would authorize, as requested, $110.4 million for development of a "conventional, prompt global strike" system designed to place a precision-guided, non-nuclear warhead on a target anywhere in the world within minutes.

The House bill also would authorize, as requested, a total of $628.3 million to develop and install various modifications in B-52, B-1, and B-2 bombers currently in service. In its report on the bill,

---

[13] In addition to the $8.08 billion currently budgeted for construction of the ship in six annual increments (FY2013-FY2018), the ship's total projected $11.4 billion cost includes $3.33 billion previously appropriated for long lead-time components in the previous six budgets (FY2007-FY2012).

---

the House Armed Services Committee expressed disappointment that DOD had budgeted less money for these bomber upgrades in FY2013 than it had projected in February 2011. The committee directed the Secretary of the Air Force to prepare a report on the advantages and disadvantages of continuing a now-cancelled upgrade of the 50-year-old B-52 fleet (designated CONECT).

The Senate committee bill would authorize the requested bomber modification funds except for $15.0 million it would cut from the $327.4 million B-2 request on grounds of unspecified "efficiencies."

Carrier-Based UAVs

Each bill would authorize a total of $264.7 million for two programs aimed at developing a long-range, stealthy drone aircraft to fly reconnaissance and attack missions from carriers. The Administration requested $142.3 million for the Unmanned Combat Air Vehicle (UCAV) project, which is intended to test the feasibility of the project, and $142.5 million for the Unmanned Carrier-launched Airborne Surveillance and Strike (UCLASS) project, which is intended to produce an operational weapon. S. 3254 would allocate funds between the two programs as requested. However, the House bill would cut $75 million from the amount requested for UCLASS and added the same amount to the request for UCAV, directing the Navy to slow the former, more operationally oriented program while it conducts additional research in the UCAS program. The panel also added to the bill a provision (Section 212) requiring the Navy to follow that course.

Ballistic Missile Defense

Congressional action on authorization of funding for selected missile defense programs is summarized in **Table A-1**. Following are some highlights.

H.R. 4310 would authorize $9.06 billion for programs managed by the Missile Defense Agency (MDA), which is $1.31 billion more than the Administration requested. More than half that increase ($680 million) would be authorized (Section 227) to be spent in FY2012-FY2017 for Israel to procure and operate its "Iron Dome" system, designed to intercept short-range rockets and artillery shells. Another major component of the House bill's increase is an addition $460 million to the amount requested for the Ground-based Midcourse Defense (GMD) anti-missile system currently based in Alaska and California, of which $103.0 million is to begin work on a third base which is to be located on the East Coast.

The Senate committee-reported bill would add $410 million to the MDA request, including no additional funds for GMD and $210.0 million for Iron Dome in FY2013.

Neither bill would authorize the $400.9 million requested to continue development of the Medium Extended Air Defense System (MEADS), a program jointly funded by the United States, Germany, and Italy to develop a mobile air and missile defense system for combat units in the field. The system would incorporate the Patriot PAC-3 missile. Plans to procure MEADS as an operational system have been shelved, but the three partner countries plan to continue the development program in hopes of harvesting technologies that could be incorporated into other systems. Under the tri-national agreement governing the program, the United States would incur significant costs if the program were terminated.

House Missile Defense Initiatives

Ground-based Midcourse Defense (GMD) System

H.R. 4310 would authorize $1.26 billion for the GMD system, an increase of $460 million over the request. Of that increase, $100 million is to begin developing a plan and a supporting environmental impact statement (required by Section 223 of the bill) to establish by the end of 2015 an anti-missile interceptor site on the East Coast. The plan is to evaluate the effectiveness, from an East Coast launch site, of various interceptor missiles including the three-stage weapon currently deployed at the existing GMD sites in Alaska and California, a two-stage version of the GMD missile, and several versions of the Navy's SM-3 Standard missile.

Another provision (Section 224) requires that, of the remaining GMD authorization increase in the bill, $205 million shall be used to begin the upgrade of the six silos in Missile Field 1 (at Ft. Greeley, AK), which the FY 2013 budget request recommends be shut down and moved to near mothball status. The provision also requires that DOD refurbish already deployed GMD interceptors.

The House bill also includes the following GMD-related provisions:

- Section 225 would require that the GMD system be tested against a target ICBM during 2013. Currently, such a test is scheduled for late 2015.

- Section 233 would require the Director, MDA, to develop a plan to increase the rate of flight and ground tests of the GMD System to ensure there are at least three such tests every two years.

- Section 222 would require that the Missile Defense Agency submit a plan to ensure that the kill vehicle for the Next Generation Aegis Missile can be adapted to also serve as an improved kill vehicle for the GMD system.

European Missile Defense

H.R. 4310 includes a provision (Section 230) that would require the Secretary of Defense and the Secretary of State to submit a plan for how the United States will share with other NATO allies the expense of a planned missile defense for Europe designated the Phased Adaptive Approach (PAA). The system, which is to incorporate land-based components of the Navy's Aegis anti-missile system using various models of the SM-3 Standard missile and AN/TPY-2 radars, is intended to intercept missiles launched from the Middle East at Europe and—eventually—at U.S. territory.

The bill would require the United States to submit to NATO a specific financing request for PAA and would prohibit the obligation of more than 25% of the funds appropriated for the program until NATO responds to the U.S. request. The President could waive that restriction if it is determined to be vital to the national security of the United States.

Missile Defense Radars

H.R. 4310 would authorize $397.4 million to buy two relocatable AN/TPY-2 missile defense radars, instead of the $$227.4 million requested to buy one. The radar is used to support the Army's THAAD anti-missile system and is planned for inclusion in the Europe-based PAA.

The bill would authorize $9.7 million, as requested, for operation of the Sea-Based X-Band Radar (SBX), a missile-detection radar mounted on a self-propelled ocean drilling platform. For FY2012, Congress had appropriated, as requested, $167 million for SBX, which was to have been based in Alaska to monitor North Korean missile launches. The FY2013 budget would downgrade the radar's mission, putting it into a semi-mothballed status from which it could be deployed either to support U.S. anti-missile tests or to observe tests of long-range North Korean missiles.

Although the House committee did not add funding to the Administration's FY2013 request for SBX, it contended that the budget was not large enough to operate the radar for an extended period either to monitor tests or to beef up the GMD missile defense system for U.S. territory. The committee ordered the director of MDA to report on the cost of keeping the radar in a state of readiness that would allow its deployment on 14 days' notice for up to 60 days per year. The committee added to the bill a provision (Section 228) requiring that SBX be maintained in such a state of readiness.

Defense Space Programs

As they had done in action on the FY2012 DOD budget, the House and Senate Armed Services Committees supported a policy of spreading across several budgets the cost of some expensive space satellites, but rejected the specific funding technique requested by DOD for that purpose. For two satellite systems, DOD proposed that Congress include in the FY2013 funding legislation provisions that would appropriate, in addition to the funds requested for FY2013, a total of $6 billion in so-called "advance appropriations" that would become available over the course of the following five years (FY2014-FY2018). According to the Air Force, this would allow a "block buy" of the two satellites, thus providing stability for the space industrial base, reducing cost, and increasing the incentive for satellite manufacturers to invest in new technologies.

In general, the congressional defense committees have not supported requests for advance appropriations because they limited Congress's oversight of programs. Instead, the committees each approved the proposed block buys, but told the Air Force to sign multi-year contracts for the satellites that the service would pay for by "incremental funding," seeking congressional approval for each year's increment of payments to the contractor in the annual budget request for that year:

- As requested, H.R. 4310 and S. 3254 each would authorize the Air Force to enter a fixed-price contract to procure two Space Based Infra-Red System (SBIRS) satellites, designed to detect the launch of long-range ballistic missiles. To buy the two satellites in a so-called block buy, the Air Force had requested authorization of $368.1 million in FY2013 and authorization of advance appropriations totaling an additional $2.50 billion to be spent in FY2014 through FY2018. Each of the bills would authorize the $368.1 million requested for SBIRS funding in FY2013 and would authorize the Air Force to sign a fixed-price contract for two satellites to be funded incrementally over a period of no more than six years.

- For two Advanced Extremely High Frequency (AEHF) Communication Satellites, the Air Force requested $557.2 million in FY2013 and planned advance procurement funding totaling $1.93 billion to be spent in FY2014-FY2017. Each of the bills would authorize the $557.2 million requested for AEHF in FY2013.

Commercial Satellite Export Rules

On May 17, 2012, the House adopted a floor amendment to H.R. 4310 that would allow the President to transfer commercial communications satellites and related components from the U.S. Munitions List, with certain reporting requirements and with prohibitions on exports to countries with which the United States maintains an arms embargo, including China (See H.Amdt. 1100, **Table 8**).

The amendment also addressed concerns that, under the current export control reform initiative, functional categories of items on the USML will be transferred to the dual-use Commerce Control List (CCL) without sufficient enumeration as to the items, parts, or components being transferred under the notification requirements of Section 38(f) of the Arms Export Control Act.[14] The amendment would require the notification to "include, to the extent practicable, an enumeration of the items or items to be removed" from the list.[15]

Operations in Iraq and Afghanistan

H.R. 4310 would authorize a total of $88.48 billion, the amount requested, for so-called Overseas Contingency Operations (OCO), that is, for operations in Iraq and Afghanistan. While the bill's total OCO authorization is the same as the total amount requested, the bill would reallocate hundreds of millions of dollars within that total.

S. 3254 would authorize $88.18 billion for OCO funding, a reduction of $300.59 million from the request. The Senate committee-reported bill would make many fewer changes in the Administration's proposed allocation of funds within the OCO total.

House Reallocations of OCO Funds

As passed by the House, H.R. 4310 would make four major additions to the Administration's OCO request that total $1.61 billion:

- $680.0 million to support Israeli purchase of the Iron Dome system, designed to intercept artillery shells and short-range rockets;

- $500.0 million to buy equipment for National Guard and reserve units;

- $200.0 million for a Defense Rapid Innovation fund; and

---

[14] The Arms Export Control Act of 1976 (Title II of P.L. 94-329) is codified in 22 U.S.C. Ch. 39.

[15] For additional information, see CRS Report R41916, *The U.S. Export Control System and the President's Reform Initiative*, by Ian F. Fergusson and Paul K. Kerr.

- $227.4 million, which the Administration requested as part of the base budget, for the Joint Improvised Explosive Device Defeat Organization (JIEDDO), a multi-service DOD agency charged with reducing the effectiveness of so-called "improvised explosive devices," which have been a major source of U.S. combat casualties in recent years.

Those four additions to the OCO budget request, plus several smaller increases, are exactly offset by reductions H.R. 4310 would make to other elements of the Administration's request. Several of these cuts would come in programs that support non-combat activity in Afghanistan and Iraq, including reductions of

- $129.0 million from the $179.0 million requested for the Task Force for Business and Stability Operations in Afghanistan;

- $200.0 million from the $400.0 million requested for the Commanders Emergency Response Program (CERP);

- $250 million from the $2.57 billion requested for depot maintenance of helicopters, vehicles, and other equipment being withdrawn from Afghanistan and Iraq (a reduction which the House Armed Services Committee justified on grounds that more work was budgeted for than could be executed);

- $650.0 million from the $1.75 billion requested for Coalition Support Funds, which reimburse certain costs incurred by countries such as Pakistan, Jordan, Mongolia, and Georgia from their support of U.S.-led efforts in Afghanistan and Iraq; and

- $25.0 million from the $400.0 million requested for the Afghan Infrastructure Fund.

The House bill also would cut a total of $280.8 million from the requests for various accounts on grounds that, historically, DOD had spent less than was appropriated for those programs.[16]

Senate Bill OCO Budget Cuts

Like the House bill, S. 3254 would transfer to the OCO accounts $227.4 million for JIEDDO, which the Administration requested as part of its base budget. However, the Senate committee bill would offset most of the increase by reducing JIEDDO funding in the OCO account by $200.0 million on grounds that the program, typically, had not spent its entire annual appropriation ("historic underexecution," in the words of the House committee report) and cutting an additional $29.0 million on grounds that the program was spending too much on service contractors.

Like the House bill, S. 3254 would authorize $200.0 million of the $400.0 million requested for CERP. The Senate bill also would cut $50.0 million from the $400.0 million requested for the Afghanistan Infrastructure Fund.

---

[16] This same argument of "historical underexecution" also was the House committee's stated justification from the $200 million reduction to the request for CERP.

Provisions Relating to Wartime Detainees

H.R. 4310 contains a subtitle addressing issues related to persons captured in the course of hostilities against Al Qaeda and associated forces, including those detained at the U.S. Naval Station at Guantanamo Bay, Cuba. Several of the provisions in H.R. 4310 would seek to extend the effect or clarify the scope of detainee provisions contained in the 2012 NDAA. The bill also would establish new restrictions on the transfer or release of detainees held by the United States in Afghanistan, establish new reporting requirements relating to detainees held on U.S. naval vessels, and, as amended, generally require that foreign terrorists accused of attacking a U.S. target be tried in a military tribunal.

The consideration and enactment of the 2012 NDAA led to significant debate regarding the extent to which U.S. persons may be detained as enemy belligerents under either the act itself or pre-existing law.[17] H.R. 4310 contains several provisions addressing this issue, including the ability of persons in military custody to seek judicial review of the legality of their detention.

The bill contains congressional findings regarding the scope of detention authority conferred by the 2001 Authorization for Use of Military Force (AUMF, P.L. 107-40) and the 2012 NDAA, the due process rights afforded to U.S. citizens placed in military detention, and the ability of U.S. citizens and persons held at Guantanamo to challenge the legality of their detention via *habeas corpus* proceedings (Sections 1031, 1032). As introduced, the bill also contained a provision specifying that nothing in the AUMF should be construed as denying the availability of *habeas* to persons detained in the United States (Section 1033). The House adopted by a vote of 243-173 an amendment to this provision to refer only to the availability of *habeas* for "persons lawfully in the United States when detained." The amended provision also requires that the executive notify Congress when such persons are placed in military detention, and permits covered detainees to file *habeas* applications within 30 days of being placed in military custody (H.Amdt. 1126, **Table 8**).

The House rejected by a vote of 182-238 an amendment to the bill (H.Amdt. 1127, **Table 8**) that would have barred indefinite military detention pursuant to the AUMF within the United States. However, it adopted by a vote of 249-171 an amendment (H.Amdt. 1105, **Table 8**) providing that, in the event that a foreign terrorist has attacked a U.S. target and may be subject to trial for the offense before a military commission, the accused may only be tried before a military commission, rather than in federal court.

H.R. 4310 also contains several provisions dealing specifically with Guantanamo detainees. It would extend through FY2013 the existing funding bar on Guantanamo detainee transfers into the United States (Section 1036), the prohibition on the use of funds to construct or modify facilities within the United States to house detainees currently held at Guantanamo (Section 1038), and, with minor modifications, the existing limitations and certification requirements relating to the transfer of Guantanamo detainees to foreign countries (Section 1037). The bill would also make minor modifications to the certification and reporting requirements contained in the 2012 NDAA relating to Guantanamo detainee transfers to foreign countries (Section 1043). The bill would

---

[17] For background, see CRS Report R42143, *The National Defense Authorization Act for FY2012: Detainee Matters*, by Jennifer K. Elsea and Michael John Garcia.

prohibit Guantanamo detainees who are "repatriated" to the Federated States of Micronesia, the Republic of Palau, or the Republic of the Marshall Islands from being able to travel to the United States (Section 1035). It would further require annual reports to be submitted to Congress regarding the recidivism of former Guantanamo detainees (Section 1039).

H.R. 1430 also contains provisions concerning detainees held abroad in locations other than Guantanamo. It would require the Secretary of Defense to submit a report regarding the use of naval vessels to detain persons pursuant to the AUMF, and would require congressional notification whenever such detention occurs (Section 1040). It would also establish certification and congressional notification requirements relating to the transfer or release of non-U.S. or Afghan nationals held by the United States at the detention facility in Parwan, Afghanistan (Section 1041), along with a report on the recidivism of former detainees who were held there (Section 1042).

The bill would extend the authority to make rewards for individuals who provide information or non-lethal assistance to the U.S. government or an ally in connection counterterrorist military operations or force protection (Section 1034).

The only detainee-related provisions of S. 3254 would extend for one year certain provisions of law adopted in prior years that otherwise would expire.

Smith-Mundt Act[18]

Section 1097 would amend and restate Section 501 of the United States Information and Educational Exchange Act of 1948 ("Smith-Mundt Act"; P.L. 80-402, 22 U.S.C. §1461) as well as Section 208 of the Foreign Relations Authorization Act, Fiscal Years 1986 and 1987 (P.L. 99-93; 22 U.S.C. §1461-1a). As currently constituted, these two provisions authorize the Secretary of State to conduct public diplomacy programs that provide information about the United States, its people, and its culture to foreign publics, but prohibit their dissemination within the United States until 12 years after the initial dissemination or preparation for dissemination of such information. Before 12 years have elapsed, Members of Congress, media organizations, and research students and scholars may examine such information. Media organizations and researchers may only examine such information at the Department of State. In addition, no funds authorized and appropriated for State Department public diplomacy programs may be used to influence public opinion in the United States.

The proposed amendments to these provisions in Section 1097 primarily would remove the prohibition on domestic dissemination of public diplomacy information produced by the Department of State and the Broadcasting Board of Governors (BBG) intended for foreign audiences, while maintaining the prohibition on using public diplomacy funds to influence U.S. public opinion.[19] Proponents of amending these two sections argue that the ban on domestic

---

[18] This section was prepared by Matthew C. Weed, Analyst in Foreign Policy Legislation.

[19] Other provisions in law would continue to prohibit the use of federal funds for "publicity and propaganda" within the United States, including Section 1031(a)(1) of the National Defense Authorization Act for Fiscal Year 2010 (Division A of P.L. 111-84, 10 U.S.C. §2241a) placing this restriction on the Department of Defense, and government-wide restrictions placed in annual appropriations acts. For a review of U.S. law regulating federal communications in the (continued...)

dissemination of public diplomacy information is impractical given the global reach of modern communications, especially the Internet, and that it unnecessarily prevents valid U.S. government communications with foreign publics due to U.S. officials' fear of violating the ban. They assert as well that lifting the ban will promote the transparency in the United States of U.S. public diplomacy and international broadcasting activities conducted abroad. Critics of lifting the ban state that it may open the door to more aggressive U.S. government activities to persuade U.S. citizens to support government policies, and might also divert the focus of State Department and the BBG communications from foreign publics, reducing their effectiveness.[20]

House Floor Amendments

Following are selected amendments on which the House took action during consideration of H.R. 4310:

Table 8. Selected House Floor Amendments to FY2013 National Defense Authorization Act (H.R. 4310)

Principal Sponsor	House Amend. Number	Summary	Disposition
		Pakistan	
Rohrabacher	H.Amdt. 1102	Prohibit funding for assistance to Pakistan in FY2013	Rejected 84-335
Connolly	H.Amdt. 1104	Withhold Coalition Support Funds from Pakistan until it allows transit of U.S. and NATO supplies in and out of Afghanistan	Agreed to 412-1
Cicilline	H.Amdt. 1139 (en bloc 5)	Condition availability of Pakistan Counterinsurgency Fund on certification that Pakistan is making significant efforts to counter the use of IEDs.	Agreed to voice vote
Flake	H.Amdt. 1143	Withhold 90% of Pakistan Counterinsurgency Fund until 30 days after Secretaries of State and Defense update report to Congress on the strategy for using those funds.	Agreed to voice vote
		Afghanistan	
Lee	H.Amdt. 1103	Provide that funds authorized for operations in Afghanistan be used only for the safe and orderly withdrawal of U.S. forces and contractors.	Rejected 113-303
DeLauro	H.Amdt. 1111 (en bloc 2)	Prohibit purchase for Afghan security forces of helicopters from any company controlled by a government that has supplied weapons to Syria or to a state sponsor of terrorism	Agreed to voice vote

(...continued)

United States, see CRS Report R42406, *Congressional Oversight of Agency Public Communications: Implications of Agency New Media Use*, by Kevin R. Kosar, and CRS Report RL32750, *Public Relations and Propaganda: Restrictions on Executive Agency Activities*, by Kevin R. Kosar.

[20] For further discussion of the Smith-Mundt Act's domestic dissemination ban, see CRS Report R40989, *U.S. Public Diplomacy: Background and Current Issues*, by Kennon H. Nakamura and Matthew C. Weed.

Principal Sponsor	House Amend. Number	Summary	Disposition
Cicilline	H.Amdt. 1139 (en bloc 5)	Condition availability of Afghan Security Forces Fund on certification that Afghanistan is "taking demonstrable steps" to recruit adequate number of personnel for Afghan Public Protection Force.	Agreed to voice vote
Iran			
Lee	H.Amdt. 1130	Create the position of Special Envoy for Iran to ensure that all diplomatic avenues are pursued to avoid a war with Iran and to prevent Iran from developing nuclear weapons.	Rejected 77-344
Conyers	H.Amdt. 1137 (en bloc 4)	Stipulate that nothing in this bill shall be construed as authorizing the use of military force against Iran.	Agreed to voice vote
Detainee Issues			
Rooney	H.Amdt. 1105	Direct DOD to hold detainee trials at the U.S. facility at Guantanamo Bay, Cuba, not in the United States.	Agreed to 249-171
Gohmert	H.Amdt. 1126	Stipulate that neither the 2001 Authorization of Military Force against Iraq nor the FY2012 National Defense Authorization Act deny any constitutional right, including habeas corpus, to anyone entitled to such rights.	Agreed to 243-173
Smith	H.Amdt. 1127	Amend the FY2012 National Defense Authorization Act to eliminate "indefinite detention" of anyone detainees by providing for immediate transfer to trial in a federal or state court.	Rejected 182-238
Strategic Weapons and Arms Control Agreements			
Markey	H.Amdt. 1109	Delay development of long-range, nuclear-armed bomber for 10 years and reduce the bill by $291.7 million, the amount it would authorize for that program, as requested	Rejected 112-308
Price	H.Amdt. 1122	Prohibit the President from making unilateral reductions to U.S. nuclear forces.	Agreed to 241-179
Johnson	H.Amdt. 1121	Require the Secretary of Defense and Chairman of the Joint Chiefs of Staff to report to Congress whether the nuclear arms reductions required by the so-called "new START" treaty are in the national security interests of the United States.	Rejected 175-245
Rehberg	H.Amdt. 1140	Prohibit elimination of any one of the three legs of the U.S. strategic nuclear "triad" (land-based ICBMs, sub-launched missiles, and bombers) and prohibit reductions to the U.S. strategic nuclear force pursuant to the "new START" treaty unless the Secretary of Defense certifies that (1) Russia is required by the treaty to make commensurate reductions; and (2) Russia is not acquiring nuclear-armed systems not covered by the treaty that could reach U.S. territory.	Agreed to 238-162
Johnson	H.Amdt. 1120	State as a "finding" of Congress that the deployment of tactical nuclear weapons to South Korea would be destabilizing and not in the U.S. national interest.	Rejected 160-261

Principal Sponsor	House Amend. Number	Summary	Disposition
Lamborn	H.Amdt. 1131	Bar the expenditure of any funds for Russia under the Cooperative Threat Reduction (CTR) program,—which is intended to dismantle weapons of mass destruction in the former Soviet—unless the Secretary of Defense certifies that Russia no longer is supporting the Syrian regime and is not assisting Syria, North Korea, or Iran in developing weapons of mass destruction. The Secretary could waive the prohibition on grounds of national security.	Agreed to voice vote
Franks	H.Amdt. 1135	Bar the expenditure of any funds for Russia under the Cooperative Threat Reduction (CTR) program,—which is intended to dismantle weapons of mass destruction in the former Soviet—unless the Secretary of Energy certifies that Russia no longer is supporting the Syrian regime and is not assisting Syria, North Korea, or Iran in developing weapons of mass destruction. The Secretary could waive the prohibition on grounds of national security.	Agreed to 241-181
Polis	H.Amdt. 1110	Reduce by $403 million the amount authorized for the Ground-based Mid-course Missile Defense (GMD) system.	Rejected 165-252
Duncan	H.Amdt. 1128	Bar the use of any funds authorized by the bill for any organization established by the United Nations in connection with the Law of the Sea (LOS) Treaty.	Agreed to 229-193

Budget Process

Principal Sponsor	House Amend. Number	Summary	Disposition
Lee	H.Amdt. 1125	Direct the President to reduce the amount authorized by this bill to be appropriated by a total of $8.231 billion.	Rejected 170-252
Rigell	H.Amdt. 1123	Replace the discretionary spending caps for FY2013 with caps equivalent to those set by the House-passed Budget Resolution (H.Con.Res. 112), contingent on the enactment of spending reductions over five years at least as large as the reductions that would have resulted from sequestration.	Agreed to 220-201
Flake	H.Amdt. 1111 (en bloc 2)	Provide that funds authorized for appropriation to pay for Overseas Contingency Operations (OCO) can be spent only on items and activities requested by the President in the OCO portion of the FY2013 budget request.	Agreed to voice vote

Other Subjects

Principal Sponsor	House Amend. Number	Summary	Disposition
McCollum	H.Amdt. 1138 (en bloc 4)	Spend no more than $200.0 million on military bands.	Agreed to voice vote
Duncan	H.Amdt. 1137 (en bloc 3)	Prohibit the use of funds for joint military exercises with Egypt if that country withdraws from its 1970 peace treaty with Israel.	Agreed to voice vote
Thornberry	H.Amdt. 1137 (en bloc 4)	Amend the Smith-Mundt Act to repeal the bar on domestic dissemination of public diplomacy material produced for dissemination to foreign audiences.	Agreed to voice vote
Price	H.Amdt. 1142	Require the Department of Justice to investigate possible violations of law regarding leaks of sensitive information about U.S. and Israeli military and intelligence capabilities.	Agreed to 379-38
Smith	H.Amdt. 1100 (en bloc 1)	Remove commercial satellites from the Munitions Control List.	Agreed to voice vote

Principal Sponsor	House Amend. Number	Summary	Disposition
Smith	H.Amdt. 1119 (en bloc 3)	Establish a Sexual Assault Oversight Council to provide independent oversight of DOD efforts to prevent and prosecute sexual assault in the armed forces.	Agreed to voice vote
Bartlett	H.Amdt. 1106	Prohibit federal agencies from requiring contractor to sign a Project Labor Agreement as a condition of winning a federal construction project.	Agreed to 211-209
Coffman	H.Amdt. 1112	Repeal the current moratorium on A-76 "contracting out" competitions.	Rejected 209-211
Wittman	H.Amdt. 1116	Require that a uniformed military chain of command, headed by a commissioned military officer, control the Army National Military Cemeteries.	Agreed to voice vote

Notes: "House Amendment Number" is the number assigned to an amendment by the House Clerk, by which amendments can be traced through CRS's Legislative Information System (LIS). It is not the same as the number assigned to the amendment by the House Rules Committee in H.Rept. 112-485, its report on the rule that governed debate on amendments to H.R. 4310 (H.Res. 661).

During floor action on the bill, dozens of amendments were aggregated into several *en bloc* amendments, each of which was agreed to by voice vote. Individual amendments in this table that were agreed to as a component of one of those en bloc amendments are so identified.

FY2013 DOD Appropriations Bill

DOD Appropriations Overview

The FY2013 DOD appropriations bill reported by the House Appropriations Committee May 25, 2012 (H.R. 5856), would provide a total of $599.89 billion for DOD activities other than military construction,[21] $3.09 billion more than the President requested. Amendments to the bill, adopted by the House on July 18-19, 2012, reduced the appropriation to $597.71 billion.

In exceeding the President's budget request—and in many of its details—the House-passed version of the DOD appropriations bill parallels H.R. 4310, the House-passed version of the companion FY2013 National Defense Authorization Act (NDAA). By the same token, the House-passed appropriation is consistent with the defense funding cap set by H.Con.Res. 112, the FY2013 budget resolution adopted by the House on March 29, 2012. Thus, it exceeds defense spending cap set by the Budget Control Act of August 2011. On those grounds, the Administration warned that the President's senior advisors would recommend that he veto the house-passed bill in its current form.[22]

---

[21] DOD's budget for the construction of facilities and the construction and operation of military family housing is funded by H.R. 5854. the FY2013 Military Construction, Veterans Affairs and Related Agencies appropriations bill. See CRS Report R42586, *Military Construction, Veterans Affairs, and Related Agencies: FY2013 Appropriations*, by Daniel H. Else, Christine Scott, and Sidath Viranga Panangala.

[22] OMB, Statement of Administration Policy on H.R. 5856, June 28, 2012.

The version of H.R. 5856 reported by the Senate Appropriations Committee on August 2, 2012, would provide $596.64 billion—$155.0 million less than the Administration's request and $1.06 billion less than the House-passed version (**Table 9**).

Table 9. FY2013 DOD Appropriations Act (H.R. 5856)

(budget authority in thousands of dollars)

	FY2012 Approp. (P.L. 112-74)	FY2013 Admin. Request	FY2013 House-Passed (H.R. 5856)	FY2013 Senate Committee-reported (H.R. 5856)
Military Personnel	131,090,539	128,430,025	128,462,794	127,502,463
Operation and Maintenance	163,073,141	174,938,933	175,103,369	170,785,490
Procurement	104,579,701	97,194,677a	102,512,191	97,635,496
Research, Development, Test & Evaluation	72,420,675	69,407,767	69,984,145	69,091,078
Revolving and Management Funds	2,675,529	2,124,320	2,080,820	2,214,024
Defense Health Program and other DOD Programs	35,593,020	35,430,579	35,905,118	35,013,758
Related Agencies	1,061,591	1,054,252	1,025,476	1,056,346
General Provisions (net)b	-2,597,704	8,000	-4,470,321	319,345
Subtotal: FY2013 Base Budget	**507,89 6,492**	**508,588,553**	**510,603,592**	**503,618,000**
Base Budget Scorekeeping Adjustments	+10,764,000	+8,057,000	+8,057,000	+8,057,000
Subtotal: Overseas Contingency Operations (OCO)	114,965,635	88,210,745	87,105,081	93,026,000
OCO Scorekeeping Adjustments	+117,000	+271,000	+271,000	+271,000
TOTAL: FY2013 DOD Appropriations	**622,862,127**	**596,799,298**	**597,708,673**	**596,644,000**
Scorekeeping Adjusted Totalc	633,743,127	605,127,298	606,036,673	604,972,000

Source: House Appropriations Committee, H.Rept. 112-493, Report on H.R. 5856, Department of Defense Appropriations Bill, FY2013, pp. 329-342; Senate Appropriations Committee, S.Rept. 112-196, Report on H.R. 5856, Department of Defense Appropriations Bill, FY2013, pp. 283-291;

Notes:

a. In addition to these funds requested for appropriation to be spent in FY2013, the Administration requested an additional $4.43 billion in so-called "advance appropriations"—funds to be spent in FY2014-FY2017. The Appropriations and Armed Services Committees of both the House and the Senate rejected the proposal for "advance appropriations," accordingly those funds are not included in the tables in this report.

b. The bulk of General Provision funding changes result from provisions that would use previously appropriated but unobligated funds for DOD's FY2013 program, thus reducing the amount of new budget authority required. For that purpose, H.R. 5856 would withdraw $2.46 billion from the Army Working Capital Fund and would rescind a total of $1.60 billion appropriated in base budget and OCO accounts for prior years.

c. The bulk of the scorekeeping adjustments are accounted for by the amounts appropriated each year by permanent law (rather than through annual appropriations bills) for the accrual contributions to the fund from which Medicare-eligible military retirees are covered under the "TRICARE-for-Life" program. The TRICARE-for-Life contributions for FY2013, which are derived from actuarial calculations, are $8.03 billion in the base budget and $271 million in the OCO account.

Proposed Administration Savings and Congressional Response

The House-passed and Senate committee-reported versions of H.R. 5856 would each add billions of dollars to the Administration's budget request—$5.5 billion in the case of the House bill—reversing some of the Administration's DOD budget reduction initiatives, summarized in **Table 10**.

In each version of the bill, that gross increase, along with other congressional initiatives summarized in **Table 11**, is partly offset by funding reductions summarized in **Table 12**.

Table 10. Administration Budget Reduction Initiatives and Congressional Reversals

Administration Proposal	House –passed H.R. 5856	Senate Committee-reported H.R. 5856
Disband 7 Air Force and Air National Guard squadrons; Retire 303 aircraft. Cancel planned procurements of Global Hawk Block 30 surveillance drones and C-27 small cargo planes. Retire those Block 30s and C-27s already purchased	Prohibits retirement or transfer to another unit of any aircraft; Adds a total of $699.2 million to budget request for Air Force, Air Force Reserve and Air National Guard to continue operations and fund 6,560 personnel slots from those three components which the Administration would eliminate. Adds $278.0 million to continue procuring and operating Global Hawk Block 30s and $140.0 million to continue operating C-27s.	Report directs DOD not to make the proposed changes until Congress receives recommendations of a Commission that would be established by the Senate version of the defense authorization bill (S 3254); Adds to the budget request $455.8 million to continue operation of the units in question and fund 9,460 personnel slots for those units. Adds $357.5 million to continue operating Global Hawk Block 30s, C-27s and A-10s which the Administration would retire.; Also requires DOD to spend funds previously appropriated for Global Hawks and C-27s
Retire four Aegis cruisers in FY2013 and three additional cruisers and two amphibious landing ships in FY2014.	Adds $602.3 million to keep in service (and modernize as earlier planned) three of the four ships. Allows retirement of the *Port Royal*, severely damaged in a 2009 grounding.	Adds $2.38 billion to man, equip, modernize (as previously planned) and operate thru FY2014 all seven cruisers and both amphibious ships the Administration would retire.

Administration Proposal	House –passed H.R. 5856	Senate Committee-reported H.R. 5856
Increase various TRICARE fees, thus reducing the FY2013 budget by $1.8 billion	Makes no change but committee says it will "continue to evaluate" the proposed changes pending action on the defense authorization bill; House-passed version of the authorization bill (H.R. 4310) would not authorize most of the proposed changes and would add $1.21 billion to the budget to replace the anticipated fee hikes. In addition, the House bill cuts $400.0 million from the $16.15 billion TRICARE request on grounds that, historically, the program has spent less than was appropriated (see also **Table 12**).	Adds to the TRICARE request 273.0 million to replace increased fees assumed in the budget. In addition, cuts $807.4 million from TRICARE request on grounds of "historic underexecution" – i.e., the program typically has spent less than was appropriated (see also **Table 12**).
Slow design of new ballistic missile submarine, reducing FY2013 funding by more than half ($640 million) from earlier projection.	n/c	n/c
Budget for one Virginia-class sub and one Aegis destroyer in FY2014 instead of two of each type (as had been planned).	Adds $723.0 million to submarine account to allow the purchase of two subs in FY2014, and $1.00 billion to allow the purchase of three destroyers rather than two (as requested) in FY2013.	Adds $777.7 million to submarine account to allow the purchase of two subs in FY2014, and $1.00 billion to allow the purchase of three destroyers rather than two (as requested) in FY2013.
Efficiencies	Adds a total of $2.11 billion to offset Administration "efficiencies" which the House committee deemed unrealistic and likely to lead to deferred maintenance of facilities.	n/a

Sources: U.S. Congress, House Committee on Appropriations, Subcommittee on Defense, *Department of Defense Appropriations Act, 2013*, report to accompany H.R. 5856, 112th Cong., 2nd sess., May 25, 2012, H.Rept. 112-493 (Washington: GPO, 2012); U.S. Congress, Senate Committee on Appropriations, Subcommittee on Department of Defense, *Department of Defense Appropriations Act, 2013*, report to accompany H.R. 5856, 112th Cong., 2nd sess., August 2, 2012, S.Rept. 112-196 (Washington: GPO, 2012).

Notes: The notation "n/c" ["no change"] signifies that no provision of the bill would block or alter the proposed policy.

Congressional Initiatives

As reported by the House Appropriations Committee, H.R. 5856 also would add to the budget request upwards of $6.0 billion for certain programs for which Congress may typically increase funding above the proposed levels:

Table 11. Selected Congressional Actions

Administration proposal	House –passed H.R. 5856	Senate Committee-reported H.R. 5856
Requests $903.0 million to continue upgrading the Ground-Based Midcourse Defense (GMD) anti-missile system deployed in Alaska and California.	Adds $75.0 million but does not order development of a third missile defense site to be located on the East Coast (as does the House-passed NDAA).	n/c
Requests $100.0 million to continue development of three Israeli missile defense systems.	Adds $168.0 million for the three Israeli systems and an additional $680.0 million for the Israeli "Iron Dome" system designed to intercept short-range rockets and artillery shells.	Adds $168.0 million for the three Israeli systems and an additional $211.0 million for the Israeli "Iron Dome" system designed to intercept short-range rockets and artillery shells.
Phases out upgrades to Abrams tanks and Bradley troop carriers, preparatory to shutting down those production lines from 2014 until 2017, when new upgrade programs would begin.	Adds $321.0 million to continue Abrams and Bradley upgrades.	Adds $165.4 million to continue Abrams upgrade.
Requests $2.04 billion for 26 F/A-18E/F Super Hornet Navy fighters and $1.03 billion for 12 EA-18G Growler electronic warfare planes (with no funds to continue Growler production in FY2014).	Adds $605.0 million for 11 additional F/A-18E/Fs and $45.0 million for long lead-time components to allow the purchase of 15 additional Growlers in FY2014.	Adds $60.0 million for long lead-time components to allow the purchase of 15 additional Growlers in FY2014.
Requests $836.6 million for seven C-130s equipped for mid-air refueling, search and rescue, and other missions.	Adds $447.0 million for seven additional C-130s equipped for various missions.	Transfers $72.0 million from Marine Corps budget request to buy two KC-130J refueling tankers (at Marine Corps request) and adds $180.0 million for components that would allow procurement of 18 C-130Js in FY2014.
Requests no funding for the National Guard and Reserve Equipment account (NGREA)	Adds $2.00 billion for the NGREA account and an additional $219.0 million for Blackhawk helicopters and $100.0 million for HMMWVs for the National Guard.	Adds $1.0 billion for the NGREA account.
Requests no funding for OCO Transfer Fund, to cover unforeseen costs of operations in Iraq and Afghanistan.	Create a $3.25 billion OCO Transfer Fund consisting of $2.0 billion cut from funds requested for Army OCO operations plus $1.25 billion added to the budget.	n/c
Within the $673.0 million requested for medical R&D, allocates no funds for specific programs for which Congress has added funds to previous budget requests.	Adds $576.4 million for 21 peer-reviewed medical R&D programs.	Allocates $354 million (within the $673.0 million requested) to increase spending for six peer-reviewed medical R&D programs.
Requests no funds for Defense Rapid Innovation Fund	Adds $250.0 million for Defense Rapid Innovation Fund	Adds $200.0 million for Defense Rapid Innovation Fund

Administration proposal	House –passed H.R. 5856	Senate Committee-reported H.R. 5856
	Adds $1.0 billion for Marine Corps "reset"—i.e., repair and reconditioning of equipment worn out by use in Afghanistan and Iraq; This increase partly offset by cut of $500.0 million to Marine Corps logistics funding on grounds of unjustified [cost] growth.	n/c

Sources: H.Rept. 112-493; S.Rept. 112-196.

Notes: The notation "n/c" ["no change"] signifies that no provision of the bill would block or alter the proposed policy.

Funding Offsets

As is customary in annual DOD appropriations bills, the House-passed and Senate committee-reported versions of H.R. 5856 would offset some of its proposed additions to the budget request with a small number of relatively large funding reductions (in addition to dozens of smaller cuts justified in terms of specific problems with specific programs).

Table 12. Selected Funding Offsets

	House –passed H.R. 5856	Senate Committee-reported H.R. 5856
Depot maintenance	Cuts $2.46 billion from the Army Working Capital Fund on grounds that Army depots have excessively large backlog of work funded in FY2012 that will carry over into FY2013.	Cuts a total of $331.7 million from the Operation and Maintenance Accounts of the four services to reduce their backlogs of depot maintenance.
TRICARE	Cuts $400.0 million from the $16.15 billion TRICARE request on grounds that the program historically underspends its annual appropriation.	Cuts $807.4 million from the request on grounds of "historical underexecution"
Requests labeled by Appropriations Committee as "unjustified," "early to need," or otherwise unnecessary	Cuts $667.5 million, including $79.4 million from funds requested for travel.	Cuts $7.35 billion (in addition to the $331.7 million depot maintenance cut and the $807.4 million TRCARE cut cited above)
Air Force spare and repair parts	Cuts $400.0 million because of excessive inventory.	n/c
Defense Acquisition Workforce Development Fund	Cuts $224.0 million from the $274.2 million requested on grounds that DOD representatives have said the requested amount would not be needed in FY2013.	Adds $445.8 million to the request, approving $720.0 million.
Medium Expanded Air Defense System (MEADS)	Cuts $400.9 million, the entire amount requested for this joint U.S-Germany-Italy program to develop a mobile anti-missile defense for units in the field.	Cut's $20.0 million, approving $380.9 million either to fund the program's final year (as the Administration proposes) or to pay the termination liability for ending the program sooner

Rescissions	Rescinds a total of $1.60 billion appropriated in prior years for specific purposes making those funds available to reduce by the same amount the requirement for new budget authority.	Rescinds a total of $3.81 billion appropriated in prior years for specific purposes making those funds available to reduce by the same amount the requirement for new budget authority.
Decommissioning the nuclear-powered aircraft carrier *Enterprise*	Cuts $470.0 million of the $940.0 million requested and requires the Navy to seek funding on a year-by-year basis.	n/c
Afghan Security Forces Fund	Cuts $722.7 million of the $5.75 billion requested on grounds that DOD has been slow in spending funds appropriated in earlier years.	Cuts $500.0 million of the $5.75 billion requested on grounds that DOD has been slow in spending funds appropriated in earlier years.
Army Operation and Maintenance [O&M] funds for war operations (Overseas Contingency Operations)	Cuts $2.00 billion cut from the Army O&M request on grounds that the budget request would have resulted in an unjustified increase in expenditures per troop)	n/c

Source: H.Rept. 112-493; S.Rept. 112-196.

Notes: The notation "n/c" ["no change"] signifies that no provision of the bill would block or alter the proposed policy.

Following are additional highlights of H.R. 5856 as passed by the House and reported by the Senate Appropriations Committee:

Military Personnel and Force Structure Appropriations

Both the version of H.R. 5856 passed by the House and the version reported by the Senate Appropriations Committee would fund the 1.7% increase in "basic pay" for military personnel proposed by the Administration. That rate is based on the Labor Department's Employment Cost Index (ECI), which is a survey-based estimate of the rate at which private-sector pay has increased.

Reduction in Personnel Transfers

A Senate committee version of the bill would cut the $2.94 billion request in the four routine personnel transfers by 10 percent ($293.6 million).[23] In its report, the committee said DOD rotates an average of one-third of military personnel from one duty station to another in any year and that the average time between such reassignments is about two years. Longer tours of duty at any one station (and, thus, fewer moves in a given year) would reduce budget costs and family stress while allowing personnel to become more proficient at any given assignment.

---

[23] This reduction would not affect the request for an additional $1.39 billion for travel costs associated with moving personnel (1) from the point of their enlistment or commissioning to their first duty station or training school, (2) from a duty station to a training school, or (3) from the last duty station to the home of record when they leave the service.

The committee directed the Under Secretary of Defense for Personnel and Readiness to send Congress, within 180 days of enactment of the FY 2013 appropriations bill, a plan for increasing the length of service members' assignments

Army, Marine Corps End-Strength Reductions

The House-passed and Senate committee-reported versions of the bill each would fund reductions in active-duty end-strength of 9,900 in the Army and 4,800 in the Marine Corps during FY2013, as proposed. In its report on the bill, however, the House Appropriations Committee expressed concern that the Administration's plan to reduce those two services by an additional 77,300 spaces by the end of FY2017 was based on budgetary pressures rather than military requirements.

Navy Cruiser Retirements

The House bill would fund continued operation during FY2013 of three of the four Aegis cruisers the Administration's budget would retire during that year. The fourth ship, USS *Port Royal*, was severely damaged in 2009 when it grounded on a coral reef off Honolulu. The bill would add to the request $124.6 million for operation and maintenance of the three other cruisers and $426.7 to upgrade their equipment (including the purchase of five MH-60R helicopters). According to the House Appropriations Committee, keeping the three ships in service allows a $2.1 million reduction in the military personnel budget request: the $36.7 million added to the request for the payroll of the three ships' crews would be more than offset by a reduction of $38.8 million to account for severance pay that would not be needed.

The Senate committee bill would add to the budget request $2.38 billion in a "Ship Modernization, Operations and Sustainment Fund" that would remain available through FY2013 and FY2014 "for the purposes of manning, operating, sustaining, equipping and modernizing" all seven of the cruisers and both of the amphibious landing ships that the Administration would retire during those two years (Section 8103).

Air Force Cuts Rejected

Like the House and Senate Armed Services Committees, the House and Senate Appropriations Committees both rejected a proposal to disband several Air Force units and mothball or dispose of nearly 300 airplanes. In its report on the bill, the House Appropriations Committee said the planned cutbacks would fall disproportionately on the Air Force Reserve and Air National Guard. Together, those two reserve components would absorb 85% of the planned reduction in airplanes and 60% of the planned manpower cuts, the committee said.

The House committee directed the Air Force to submit by October 1, 2012, a cost-benefit analysis of the proposed retirements and reorganizations that is to be reviewed by the Government Accountability Office (GAO).

The House bill's military personnel accounts would add $120.8 million to the budget request to cover the cost of 560 active-duty Air Force personnel, 900 members of the Air Force Reserve, and 5,100 members of the Air National Guard who would be dropped from the rolls under the Administration's proposal.

The Senate committee-reported version of the bill would add to the request a total of $455.8 million to continue operation of the units in question and fund 9,460 personnel slots for those units. It also would add to the FY2013 request a total of $357.5 to continue operating the Global Hawk Block 30s, C-27s and A-10s that the Administration would retire. A provision of the Senate committee bill (Section 8110) would require DOD to spend funds previously appropriated for procurement of Global Hawk Block 30s and C-27s.

In its report, the Senate committee directs DOD not to carry out the proposed changes until Congress receives recommendations of a commission that would be established by the Senate version of the defense authorization bill (S. 3254).

Defense Secretary Leon Panetta and Air Force Secretary Michael Donley have said that they will defer action on the proposed changes pending congressional action on the issue.

Depot Maintenance 'Carryover'

The House-passed and Senate Appropriations Committee-reported versions of H.R. 5856 each would cut the Administration's budget request in an effort to reduce what the committees deemed to be an excessive backlog of scheduled maintenance work by the services' depots, which perform major overhauls of aircraft, ground vehicles, engines, electronic equipment and other major items. Essentially, the committees took the position that they would reduce the amount of additional funds appropriated for overhauls in FY2013 while the depots would keep working at their regular temple, drawing down the backlogs.

The issue, which the GAO has been scrutinizing for years, is referred to as "excess carryover" and is described by a July 2008 GAO report on Army depots:

> The five Army depots operate under the working capital fund concept, where customers are to be charged for the anticipated full cost of goods and services. To the extent that the depots do not complete work at [sic–apparently means "by"] year-end, the funded work will be carried into the next fiscal year. Carryover is the reported dollar value of work that has been ordered and funded (obligated) by customers but not completed by working capital fund activities at the end of the fiscal year. The congressional defense committees recognize that some carryover is needed to ensure a smooth flow of work during the transition from one fiscal year to the next. However, past congressional defense committee reports raised concerns that the level of carryover may be more than is needed. Excessive amounts of carryover financed with customer appropriations are subject to reductions by the Department of Defense (DOD) and the congressional defense committees during the budget review process.[24]

The House-passed version of H.R. 5856 includes a provision (Section 8087) that would cut a total of $2.46 billion from the amounts requested for Army Operation and Maintenance (O&M) and for the Army's Other Procurement accounts, explaining the action in a summary table as, "Excess Working Capital Fund Carryover." Citing the same rationale, the Senate committee-reported

---

[24] U.S. Government Accountability Office, Army Working Capital Fund: Actions Needed to Reduce Carryover at Amry Depots, GAO-08-714, July 2008, pp. 1-2.

version of the bill would cut a total of $331.7 million from the amounts requested for the O&M accounts of the four armed services.

TRICARE Fee Increases and Cost Savings

Proposed TRICARE Fee Increases

The Administration's $16.15 billion request for the TRICARE medical insurance program that covers active and retired service members, their dependents, and their survivors assumed certain increases in various fees paid by participants. While some of those proposed increases are allowed by current law, most of them would require new legislation. The House-passed and Senate committee-reported versions of the FY2013 defense authorization bill would reject several of those proposed changes.

As reported by the House Appropriations Committee, H.R. 5856 incorporates the TRICARE cost savings that would result from the Administration's proposed fee hikes. In its report on the bill, the House Committee said it would "continue to evaluate the proposed changes," pending enactment of the companion defense authorization bill.

The Senate committee's version of the bill would add $273.0 million to the request to cover higher than budgeted costs should Congress reject some of the proposed TRICARE fee increases.

TRICARE Savings Assumed

Citing the Government Accountability Office (GAO) as its authority, the Senate Appropriations Committee said, in its report on H.R. 5856, that the TRICARE program had "underexecuted" its budget (i.e., had spent less than was appropriated) by $771.6 million in FY2010 and by $1.36 billion in FY2011, and that it was on track to spend $1.04 billion less than had been appropriated for FY2012. On the assumption thtat this pattern of "historic underexecution" would continue in FY2013, the Senate committee's version of the defense bill would cut $807.4 million from the FY2013 TRICARE request, a reduction of 5 percent.

The House-passed version of the bill would cut $400.0 million from the TRICARE budget request on grounds of "historic underexecution."

Ground Combat Systems Appropriations

Congressional action on appropriation of funds for selected ground combat systems is summarized in **Table A-4**. Following are some highlights.

Abrams Tank and Bradley Upgrades; Hercules tank recovery vehicles

The budget requested $74.4 million to support the fielding of M-1 tanks for which previous budgets had funded conversion to the "M-1A2SEP" version, which incorporates improvements to the power train, communications gear, and night-vision equipment. The House-passed version of H.R. 5856 would increase the request by $188.0 million, to upgrade additional M-1s to the A2SEP standard.

The House bill also would add $140.0 million to the $148.2 million requested to upgrade Bradley armored troop carriers. The additional funds would be used to equip the vehicles with improved digital communications systems and night-vision equipment.

In addition, the House bill would add $62.0 million to the $107.9 million requested for M-88A2 Hercules tank recovery vehicles – tracked vehicles designed to tow to safety a disabled 70-ton Abrams tank.

The Senate committee version of H.R. 5856 would add $91.0 million to the Abrams tank upgrade request, $123.0 million to the tank recovery vehicle request, and no funds to the Bradley upgrade request.

Overall Combat Vehicle Modernization Plan

The House-passed and Senate committee versions of H.R. 5856 both would provide $639.9 million, as requested, to continue development of the Ground Combat Vehicle (GCV), which is intended to replace the Bradley armored troop carrier. However, in its report on the bill, the Senate Appropriations Committee questioned the emphasis the Army was placing on that project considered in the context of its overall spending plans for modernization of its armored combat vehicle fleet.

Under current Army plans, the Senate committee said, the GCV would account for about 10 percent of the Army's entire fleet of combat vehicles. In the FY2013 budget request, it accounts for more than 70 percent of the total amount requested for modernization of the ground combat fleet. Over the five-year period FY2013-FY2017, GCV would absorb more than 80 percent of the service's projected spending on combat vehicle modernization. The committee directed the Army to provide to Congress the results of a business case analysis—currently underway—of its combat vehicle fleet modernization plans.

Naval Systems Appropriations

In their respective reports on H.R. 5856, the Appropriations Committees of both the House and Senate decried the Administration's plan to reduce the number of warships projected for funding in FY2013-FY2017 compared with the Navy's previous five-year plan. Both committees warned that the projected reduction in shipbuilding would increase costs and weaken the nation's shipbuilding industrial base. The House committee also contended that the Administration's plan was inconsistent with its increased emphasis on U.S. military power in the Pacific region, where naval forces would play a particularly significant role.

Congressional action on appropriation of funds for selected naval systems is summarized in **Table A-6**. Following are highlights.

Submarine and Destroyer Production

Like the Armed Services Committees of the House and Senate, the House and Senate Appropriations Committee objected to the Administration's plan to buy one Virginia-class attack submarine and one Aegis destroyer in FY2014, rather than two ships of each type, as had been planned. "The Navy has approached the committee with various plans and schemes to attempt to restore these ships to FY2014," the House Appropriations Committee said in its report on H.R. 5856.

All four of the congressional defense committees argued for providing enough funds in FY2013 to support multi-year contracts to procure 10 submarines and 10 destroyers in order to realize cost-cutting efficiencies.

The House-passed version of H.R. 5856 would add to the request $723 million in long lead-time funding to buy components that allow the Navy to start two submarines rather than one in FY2014. The bill also would include an additional $1.0 billion to fund a third destroyer in FY2013, in addition to the two requested, stating in its report that the "Secretary of the Navy is directed to use this funding as part of the DDG-51 multiyear procurement planned for fiscal years 2013 through 2017 in order to achieve a lower cost and provide a more stable production base for the duration of the DDG-51 multiyear procurement."[25] In its report, the House committee rejected Navy proposals to squeeze the additional ships into the currently projected shipbuilding budgets by funding them "incrementally"—appropriating for each fiscal year only the amount that would be spent in that year—rather than following the usual policy of "full-funding," under which the full cost of any ship would have to be appropriated for a single year.[26]

The Senate committee's version of H.R. 5856 would add to the budget $777.7 million—about 7.6 percent more than the House-passed version—for components to allow procurement of a second submarine in FY 2014. For the additional destroyer, the Senate committee bill would add the same amount as the House bill—$1.0 billion.

The Senate committee bill includes a provision (Section 8010) that would authorize incremental funding for additional submarines—an approach the House committee had rejected. But the Senate committee took a more cautious approach in approving modifications to proven ship designs:

- The Senate committee cut $90.0 million from the $100.0 million requested to develop the "Virginia Payload Module"—a 94 foot-long hull section intended to be inserted into the Virginia-class design to carry additional weapons, unmanned mini-subs and other equipment. In its report, the committee said it was unclear that the proposed addition would not disrupt submarine production and compromise the ships' performance.

- The Senate committee also insisted that destroyers built under the planned multi-year contract not incorporate a powerful new radar, currently under development, to improve the ships' anti-missile defense capability. Like the House-passed version of H.R. 5856, the Senate committee version would provide the $223.6 million requested to continue development of this Air and Missile Defense Radar (AMDR). However, the Senate committee said it would be premature to include the new radar in the ships to be purchased under the pending multi-year contract.

---

[25] "DDG-51" identifies the Arleigh Burke class of destroyers currently being procured by the Navy.

[26] CRS Report RL31404, *Defense Procurement: Full Funding Policy—Background, Issues, and Options for Congress*, by Ronald O'Rourke and Stephen Daggett.

USS **Miami** *Fire Damage Repair*

The Senate committee version of H.R. 5856 would add to the budget $150 million for the repair of the Virginia-class submarine USS *Miami*, damaged by fire on May 23, 2012, and undergoing an overhaul at the Portsmouth Naval Shipyard in Kittery, Maine. On August 22, 2012, the Navy announced that it plans to repair the ship, at an estimated cost of $450.0 million, by April 30, 2015, after which the ship would be good for an additional 10 years of service.[27]

The anticipated unit-cost of one Virginia-class submarine in the FY2013 budget is $2.55 billion.

Amphibious Transport Dock (LPD-17)

In its report on the bill, the Senate Appropriations Committee noted that the Navy has fewer amphibious landing transports than current DOD plans call for and that the number of such ships is slated to decline further. To stem that decline, the committee added to the request $263.3 million for long leadtime components to be used in an LPD-17-class amphibious transport dock ship to be purchased in FY2014.

Afloat Forward Staging Base (AFSB)

In its FY2013 appropriations submission, the Navy requested $38.0 million to purchase certain components in advance of ordering a ship purpose-built as a mobile at-sea platform to support and sustain various maritime operations. The vessel, known as the Afloat Forward Staging Base (AFSB), would be a modification of an existing ship type, the Mobile Landing Platform (MLP), that is currently under construction. The House-passed bill denied the requested funding, while the Senate committee version granted the request and added to it $106.5 million of budget authority.

The MLP program is designed to give the Navy the ability to transfer rolling stock, such as trucks and Humvees, at sea between ships that lack the capability to offload such cargo without port facilities. It does so by providing a very low, flat deck area onto which both vehicles can drive from their transport ships using ramps and Navy air cushion landing craft (LCACs) can "fly" under their own power. Once aboard, the vehicles can be loaded onto the LCACs for transfer to amphibious assault ships to join with the Marines who will use them in operations. The Navy has planned to build three such MLPs and has already received much of the necessary funding.

Over the past several years, the Navy has weighed its need for MLPs against the need for additional offshore capabilities. The Afloat Forward Staging Base (AFSB) would adapt the MLP platform to become a floating base for smaller vessels (e.g., minesweepers or patrol craft) and helicopters that could perform a variety of missions. After having concluded that two MLPs will satisfy the cargo transfer requirement, the Navy proposed using the requested FY2013 MLP funding to begin the process of converting the third MLP into an AFSB and indicated that funding

---

[27] Navy News Service, "Navy Provides Updated Cost Estimate for USS *Miami* Repair," August 22, 2012, accessed at http://www.navy.mil/submit/display.asp?story_id=69153.

for a fourth MLP, purpose-built as an AFSB, would be requested for FY2014. The requested $38.0 million was intended to procure the initial components that would go into that fourth MLP.

As noted, the House-passed version of H.R. 5856 denied all funding for this purpose, instructing the Navy to instead modify existing ships as necessary to fulfill specific missions and to apply the AFSB funding planned for FY2014 toward the submarine construction program.

The Senate committee reacted differently to the proposal. The committee recommended that the request to redirect the $38.0 million of advance procurement for the fourth MLP into the conversion of the the third ship into an AFSB be granted and that an additional $97.0 million be provided in FY2013 in order to complete the task.

> For a fuller discussion of the Navy shipbuilding program, see CRS Report RL32665, *Navy Force Structure and Shipbuilding Plans: Background and Issues for Congress*, by Ronald O'Rourke.

Aircraft Appropriations

Congressional action on appropriation of funds for selected aircraft and long-range strike programs is summarized in **Table A-10**. Following are some highlights:

F-35 Joint Strike Fighter

H.R. 5856 would appropriate 95% of the $8.69 billion requested to continue development and production of the F-35 Joint Strike Fighter. The bill would provide $5.59 billion to buy a total of 29 planes of three types: a carrier-based version for the Navy, a short-takeoff version for the Marine Corps, and a conventional, land-based version for the Air Force. The bill also would provide $2.68 billion to continue development of the plane.

F-22 Oxygen System

The House bill would add $50.0 million to the $283.9 million requested for modifications to the Air Force's F-22 fighters, with the additional funds intended to install a backup oxygen supply for the pilots in each aircraft. The Air Force has been investigating complaints by some F-22 pilots that they have experienced symptoms similar to those caused by hypoxia (oxygen deprivation). While the Air Force has not concluded its inquiry, there has been speculation that the system installed in the planes to provide oxygen to the pilot may be at fault.

C-130 Cargo Planes

H.R. 5856 would add to the request $447.0 million for seven C-130 cargo planes, most of which would be equipped for specialized missions such as mid-air refueling and search-and-rescue. In its report, the House committee noted that the Air Force had previously announced plans to buy 12 C-130s in FY2013 and that the FY2012 defense appropriations act had provided $120.0 million to buy components that would be needed to permit the purchase of 12 planes in FY2013.

The bill also would add $20.0 million to the Air Force's procurement and R&D accounts to continue the C-130 Avionics Modernization Program (AMP), a project to upgrade the cockpit electronics of older planes. The Administration's budget would scrap the program.

Military aircraft programs are explained in detail in reports written by Jeremiah Gertler, Specialist in Military Aviation, that are available to congressional clients through the CRS website.

Missile Defense Appropriations

The House-passed version of H.R. 5856 would appropriate $9.06 billion for programs of the Missile Defense Agency, a 17% increase above the $7.75 billion request. Nearly two-thirds of the increase is accounted for by the House committee's addition of $848 million for four Israeli missile defense systems, which includes $680 million for the Iron Dome system designed to intercept short-range rockets and artillery shells.

The version of the defense bill reported by the Senate Appropriations Committee would add $587 million to the Missile Defense Agency budget request.

Congressional action on appropriation of funds for selected missile defense programs is summarized in **Table A-2**. Following are some highlights.

Ground-Based Missile Defense (GMD) System

For the Ground-Based Missile Defense (GMD) system currently deployed at sites in Alaska and Hawaii, the House-passed bill would provide $978.2 million, an increase of $75 million over the request. In the House committee's report on H.R. 5856, the stated rationale for the increase was "sustainment."

The House version of the defense appropriations bill was silent on the provisions of the House version of the companion defense authorization bill directing DOD to spend $100.0 million to begin work on deploying additional anti-missile interceptors at a third site on the East Coast of the United States.

The Senate committee version of the bill would provide the $903.2 million requested for GMD.

Medium Extended Air Defense System (MEADS)

H.R. 5856 would provide none of the $400.9 million requested to continue development of the Medium Extended Air Defense System (MEADS), a joint U.S.-German-Italian effort to develop a mobile air and missile defense system that incorporates the Patriot PAC-3 missile, which is designed to protect combat units in the field.

Plans to deploy MEADS have been shelved, but the three partner countries are continuing work on the system in hopes of developing components and technologies that could be used in other systems. Under the tripartite Memorandum of Understanding governing the program, the United States would incur significant cash penalties if it unilaterally pulled out of the program. The House-passed version of the appropriations bill would deny all funding for MEADS.

In its official Statement of Administration Position on the bill, OMB said it "strongly objects," stating

> There is a high likelihood that this action would be perceived by our partners, Italy and Germany, as breaking our commitment under the Memorandum of Understanding. This

could harm our relationship with our allies on a much broader basis, including future multinational cooperative projects. It also could prevent the completion of the agreed [test activities] necessary to harvest technology from U.S. and partner investments in MEADS.[28]

In its report, the House committee acknowledged that additional funding might yield some benefits, but added: "The expected benefits do not justify the cost."[29]

The Senate committee version of the bill would provide $380.9 million that could be used either to complete the MEADS development program or to pay the fee the U.S. government would incur through termination. In its report on the bill, the Senate committee said the costs would be about the same in either case.[30]

> CRS reports written by Stephen A. Hildreth, Specialist in Missile Defense, cover these issues in detail.

OCO Funding: Afghanistan and Related Activities

The House-passed version of H.R. 5856 would provide $87.11 billion for Overseas Contingency Operations (OCO)—basically, operations in Afghanistan and Iraq and supporting activities, which is $1.11 billion less than the request. The Senatecommittee-reported version of the bill would provide $93.03 billion for OCO funding, $4.82 billion more than the request.

Table 13. OCO Funding Highlights in FY 2013 DOD Appropriations Bill (H.R. 5856)

Issue	House-passed H.R. 5856	Senate Committee-reported H.R. 5856
Funds requested in the Base Budget, funded in Title IX (OCO funds), which is currently exempt from budget caps	Transfer $3.54 billion total to Title IX	Transfer $6.55 billion to Title IX
$5.75 billion requested for Afghan Security Forces Fund	Cut $723 million	Cut $600 million
$400 million requested for Commanders Emergency Response Program (CERP)	Cut $200 million	Cut $200 million
Rescissions of OCO funds provided by prior appropriations	Cut $580 million	Cut $1.71 billion
$1.75 billion requested for Coalition Support Fund	Floor amendment cut $650 million	n/c
O&M requests deemed by the committee to be unjustified	Cut $2.0 billion from Army O&M and $500 million from Marine Corps O&M	n/c

---

[28] OMB, Statement of Administration Policy on H.R. 5856, June 28, 2012.

[29] H.Rept. 112-493, p. 219.

[30] S.Rept. 112-196, p. 179.

Issue	House-passed H.R. 5856	Senate Committee-reported H.R. 5856
Additional funds to "resed" equipment returned to U.S. after service in Iraq and Afghanistan	Add $1.00 billion	Transfer $1.13 billion from Army base budget request and $110 million from Marine Corps base budget request (included in the $6.55 billion transfer total noted above)
Additional ship deployments to Central Command region	n/c	Add $293 million

Source: H.Rept. 112-493; S.Rept. 112-196.

Notes: The notation "n/c" ["no change"] signifies that no provision of the bill would block or alter the proposed policy.

Aid to Pakistan

In the official Statement of Administration Policy, OMB objected to a provision of the House committee bill that would impose limitations on payments to Pakistan from the $1.75 billion Coalition Support Fund. The payments from the fund are intended to reimburse U.S. coalition partners—chiefly Pakistan and Jordan—for expenses they incur from supporting U.S. military operations in Afghanistan and Iraq.

As reported by the House Appropriations Committee, H.R. 5856 would have provided the $1.75 billion requested for CSF. However, Section 9015 of the bill would have barred any payments from the fund to Pakistan (slated to receive $1.30 billion) unless the Secretaries of Defense and State certify that the government of Pakistan is cooperating with U.S. policy in certain respects, including supporting counterterrorism operations against al Qaeda and certain other groups with bases in Pakistan.

An amendment adopted during House debate on H.R. 5856 cut $650 million from the CSF request, with the intent of cutting Pakistan's payment by 50 percent to $650 million.

Detainee Issues

OMB also said it "strongly objects" to several provisions of the House-passed version of H.R. 5856 restricts the transfer to any other location those detainees who are neither U.S. citizens nor members of the U.S. Armed Forces and are held in the U.S. facility at Guantanamo Bay, Cuba. Three provisions of H.R. 5856 at issue are

- Section 8108, which would prohibit the transfer to (or release within) U.S. territory of any such detainee;

- Section 8109, which would prohibit the transfer to any other country of any such detainee except to a country where the host government would likely retain the detainee in custody and render him unable to threaten U.S. interests; and

- Section 8110, which would prohibit the use of any funds to build, acquire, or modify any facility in U.S. territory to house Guantanamo detainees.

The Senate committee-reported version of H.R. 5856 contains analogous provisions in Sections 8105, 8106 and 8107, respectively.

House Floor Amendments

Following are selected amendments on which the House took action during consideration of H.R. 5856:

Table 14. Selected House Floor Amendments to FY 2013 DOD Appropriations Act (H.R. 5856)

Principal Sponsor	House Amend. Number[a]	Summary[b]	Disposition
Overall Budget Reduction Proposals			
Woolsey	1404	Cut the total appropriated by $181 million, the amount by which the House-passed Transportation Department Appropriation Bill (H.R. 5972) would reduce funding for the Federal Transit Administration.	Rejected voice vote
Woolsey	1406	Cut the total appropriated by $294 million, the amount by which the Labor-HHS Appropriations bill drafted by a House Appropriations subcommittee would reduce funding for Title X Family Planning programs.	Rejected 106-311
Woolsey	1411	Cut the total appropriated by $1.7 billion, the annual budget for the Social Services Block Grant Program, which the House Ways and Means committee voted to eliminate as part of the FY2013 budget process.	Rejected 91-328
Lee	1419	Cut the total appropriated by $19.2 billion, reducing it to the amount appropriated for DOD in FY2008.	Rejected 87-326
Lee	1421	Cut the total appropriated by $7.58 billion, an amount that would reduce DOD appropriations as required by the 2011 Budget Control Act.	Rejected 171-243
Mulvaney	1431	Cut the total appropriated by $1.07 billion, an amount that would freeze DOD appropriations at the FY2012 level (except for personnel, health care, and war costs).	Agreed to 247-167
Specific Budget Cuts			
McCollum	1378	Cut $188 million to reduce spending on military bands.	Rejected 166-250
Kingston	1380	Cut $27 million to eliminate recruiting advertising on NASCAR racers.	Rejected 202-216
Quigley	1391	Cut $988 million to eliminate an Aegis destroyer the bill would add to the budget.	Rejected 60-359
Cohen	1392	Cut $507 million the bill would add to retain for Aegis cruisers the Administration would retire; Add $235 million for additional Cancer research.	Rejected 145-273
Pompeo	1393	Cut $250 million to eliminate the Rapid Innovation Fund.	Rejected 137-282
Medical R&D Additions			
Kucinich	1383	Shift $10 million to research on treatment of Gulf War Syndrome.	Agreed voice vote
Langevin	1386	Shift $15 million to research on spinal cord injury	Agreed voice vote
Session	1387	Shift $10 million to research on Traumatic Brain Injury and Post-Traumatic Stress Disorder	Agreed voice vote

Principal Sponsor	House Amend. Number[a]	Summary[b]	Disposition
Walz	1388	Shift $10 million to research on vision and eye disorders	Agreed voice vote
Boswell	1402	Shift $10 million to suicide prevention efforts	Agreed voice vote
		Reductions to Afghanistan-related Costs	
Jones	1397	Cut $412 million from incentive pay for Afghan Security Forces and add $149 million for incentive pay for U.S. personnel	Agreed voice vote
Ciciline	1400	Cut $375 million from the Afghan Infrastructure Fund (thus eliminating the fund).	Rejected 149-270
Cohen	1401	Cut $175 million from the Afghan Infrastructure Fund.	Agreed 228-191
Poe	1412	Cut $650 million from Coalition Support Funds (thus cutting by 50 percent the projected aid to Pakistan).	Agreed voice vote
Lee	1414	Cut $20.8 billion from the request for Overseas contingency Operation (OCO) costs, with the aim of requiring withdrawal of U.S. forces from Afghanistan.	Rejected 107-312
Garamendi	1430	Cut $20.8 billion from the request for Overseas Contingency Operation (OCO) costs, with the aim of requiring a continuing drawdown of U.S. forces in Afghanistan during FY2014.	Rejected 137-278
Strategic Nuclear Weapons-related Issues			
Markey	1394	Cut $75 million the bill would add to the budget for Ground-Based Missile Defense.	Rejected 150-268
Markey	1405	Prohibit the use of funds to deploy more than 300 ICBMs.	Rejected 136-283
Turner	1424	Prohibit the use of funds to make certain reductions in nuclear weapons.	Agreed 235-178
Berg	1427	Prohibit any reduction in the number of certain types of nuclear weapons delivery vehicles.	Agreed 233-183
Other Issues			
Amash	1395	Remove Section 8039 (which restricts the contracting-out to private firms of functions performed by federal employees).	Rejected 186-233
King	1415	Exempt military construction projects from the Davis-Bacon Act.	Rejected 82-235
King	1416	Prohibit the use of funds to violate the Defense of Marriage Act.	Agreed 247-166
Coffman	1426	Mandate by law the Administration's decision to withdraw two Army brigade combat teams from Europe.	Rejected 123-292
Stearns	1435	Prohibit the introduction of any new fee for TRICARE-for-Life.	Agreed 399-117

Notes:

a. "House Amendment Number" is the number assigned to an amendment by the House Clerk, by which amendments can be traced through the CRS Legislative Information System (LIS).

b. In many cases, the proposed amendment would add or cut a specific amount to an appropriations account without specifying the intended purpose. In those cases, the intent of the amendment is determined by the proponents' statements during debate on the proposal. The cost estimates implicit in these amendment cummaries reflect the assertions of the amendment sponsors and have not been verified by CRS.

Appendix A. Selected Program Funding Tables

Table A-1. Congressional Action on Selected FY2013 Missile Defense Funding Authorization

(amounts in millions of dollars)

PE Number (for R&D projects only)	Program Element Title	FY2013 Administration Request	House-Passed Authorization	Senate Committee-Reported Authorization	Conference Report	Comments
0603175C	BMD Technology	79,975	79,975	79,975		
0603274C	Special Programs	36,685	36,685	36,685		
0603881C	BMD Terminal Defense Segment	316,929	316,929	316,929		
0603882C	BMD Midcourse Defense Segment	903,172	1,363,172	903,172		System based in Alaska and California to defend U.S. territory; House added $103 million to add a launch site on the East Coast plus $357 million to otherwise expand the program
0603884C	BMD Sensors	347,012	347,012	347,012		
0603890C	BMD Enabling Programs	362,711	362,711	362,711		
0603891C	Special Programs	272,387	272,387	272,387		
0603892C	AEGIS BMD	992,407	992,407	992,407		
0603893C	Space Tracking & Surveillance System	51,313	51,313	51,313		
0603895C	BMD System Space Programs	6,912	6,912	6,912		
0603896C	BMD Command and Control, Battle Management and Communications	366,552	366,552	366,552		
0603898C	BMD Joint Warfighter Support	55,550	55,550	55,550		

PE Number (for R&D projects only)	Program Element Title	FY2013 Administration Request	House-Passed Authorization	Senate Committee-Reported Authorization	Conference Report	Comments
0603901C	Directed Energy Research	46,944	76,944	46,944		House added funds to accelerate development of anti-missile lasers
0603902C	Aegis SM-3 Block IIB	224,077	224,077	224,077		
0603904C	Missile Defense Integration & Operations Center (MDIOC)	63,043	63,043	63,043		
0603906C	Regarding Trench	11,371	11,371	11,371		
0603907C	Sea-Based X-Band Radar (SBX)	9,730	9,730	9,730		
0603913C	Israeli Cooperative Programs	99,836	267,836	199,836		
	Iron Dome	0.0	680,000	210,000		
0603914C	BMD Tests	454,400	454,400	454,400		
0603915C	BMD Targets	435,747	435,747	435,747		
0604880C	Land-based SM-3	276,338	276,338	276,338		
0604881C	Aegis SM-3 Block IIA Co-Development	420,630	420,630	420,630		
0604883C	Precision Tracking Space System (PTSS)	297,375	50,000	297,375		
0604886C	Advanced Remote Sensor Technology	58,742	58,742	58,742		
0901598C	Management HQ-MDA	34,855	34,855	34,855		
Subtotal, MDA RDT&E,		**6,224,693**	**7,315,318**	**6,534,693**		
THAAD, Fielding		460,728	587,728	560,728		36 interceptors requested; House adds 12
Aegis BMD		389,626	389,626	389,626		29 interceptors requested;
AN/TPY-2 radar		217,244	387,244	217,244		One radar requested; House adds one

PE Number (for R&D projects only)	Program Element Title	FY2013 Administration Request	House- Passed Authorization	Senate Committee-Reported Authorization	Conference Report	Comments
Subtotal, MDA Procurement		**1,077,775**	**1,374,775**	**1,177,775**		
	THAAD, O&M	55,679	55,679	55,679		
	Aegis BMD O&M	12,163	12,163	12,163		
	Ballistic Missile Defense Radars. O&M	192,133	192,133	192,133		
Subtotal, MDA, O&M		**259.975**	**259,975**	**259,975**		
	Aegis Ashore Site, Romania	157,900	82,900	157,900		
	Midcourse Defense Data Link, Fort Drum, N.Y.	25,900	25,900	25,900		
	Planning & Design	4,548	4,548	4,548		
Subtotal, MDA, Military Construction		**188,348**	**113,348**	**188,348**		
Total, Missile Defense Agency		**7,750,791**	**9,063,417**	**8,160,791**		
0604869A	Medium Extended Air Defense System (MEADS)	400,861	0.0	0.0		
0102419A	Aerostat Joint Project Office	190,422	171,422	190,422		
Selected Army R&D missile defense		**591,283**	**171,422**	**190,422**		
	Patriot Missile (PAC-3) procurement	646,590	696,590	646,590		84 interceptors requested; House added funds for unspecified additional number
Total, Selected Army Missile Defense		**1,237,873**	**868,012**	**837,012**		
Grand Total, Missile Defense		**8,988,664**	**9,931,429**	**8,997,803**		

Table A-2. Congressional Action on Selected FY2013 Missile Defense Funding Appropriation

(amounts in millions of dollars)

PE Number (for R&D projects only)	Program Element Title	FY2013 Administration Request	House-Passed Appropriation	Senate Committee-Reported Appropriation	Conference Report	Comments
0603175C	BMD Technology	79,975	75,975			
0603274C	Special Programs	36,685	36,685			
0603881C	BMD Terminal Defense Segment	316,929	296,929			
0603882C	BMD Midcourse Defense Segment	903,172	978,172			System based in Alaska and California to defend U.S. territory; House added $103 million to add a launch site on the East Coast plus $357 million to otherwise expand the program
0603884C	BMD Sensors	347,012	347,012			
0603890C	BMD Enabling Programs	362,711	362,711			
0603891C	Special Programs	272,387	272,387			
0603892C	AEGIS BMD	992,407	992,407			
0603893C	Space Tracking & Surveillance System	51,313	51,313			
0603895C	BMD System Space Programs	6,912	6,912			
0603896C	BMD Command and Control, Battle Management and Communications	366,552	341,552			
0603898C	BMD Joint Warfighter Support	55,550	55,550			
0603901C	Directed Energy Research	46,944	41,944			
0603902C	Aegis SM-3 Block IIB	224,077	204,077			

PE Number (for R&D projects only)	Program Element Title	FY2013 Administration Request	House-Passed Appropriation	Senate Committee-Reported Appropriation	Conference Report	Comments
0603904C	Missile Defense Integration & Operations Center (MDIOC)	63,043	63,043			
0603906C	Regarding Trench	11,371	11,371			
0603907C	Sea-Based X-Band Radar (SBX)	9,730	9,730			
0603913C	Israeli Cooperative Programs	99,836	267,836			
	Iron Dome	0.0	680,000			
0603914C	BMD Tests	454,400	454,400			
0603915C	BMD Targets	435,747	435,747			
0604880C	Land-based SM-3	276,338	266,338			
0604881C	Aegis SM-3 Block IIA Co-Development	420,630	420,630			
0604883C	Precision Tracking Space System (PTSS)	297,375	242,375			
0604886C	Advanced Remote Sensor Technology	58,742	33,742			
0901598C	Management HQ-MDA	34,855	34,855			
Subtotal, MDA RDT&E,		**6,224,693**	**7,315,318**			
	THAAD, Fielding	460,728	460,728			
	Aegis BMD	389,626	389,626			
	AN/TPY-2 radar	217,244	217,244			
Subtotal, MDA Procurement		**1,077,775**	**1,374,775**			
	THAAD, O&M	55,679	55,679			
	Aegis BMD O&M	12,163	12,163			
	Ballistic Missile Defense Radars. O&M	192,133	192,133			

PE Number (for R&D projects only)	Program Element Title	FY2013 Administration Request	House-Passed Appropriation	Senate Committee-Reported Appropriation	Conference Report	Comments
Subtotal, MDA, O&M		**259.975**	**259,975**			
	Aegis Ashore Site, Romania	157,900	82,900			MDA Military Construction Projects are funded in H.R. 5854, the FY2013 Military Construction, Veterans Affairs and Related Agencies Appropriations Bill.
	Midcourse Defense Data Link, Fort Drum, N.Y.	25,900	25,900			
	Planning & Design	4,548	4,548			
Subtotal, MDA, Military Construction		**188,348**	**113,348**			
Total, Missile Defense Agency		**7,750,791**	**9,063,417**			
0604869A	Medium Extended Air Defense System (MEADS)	400,861	0.0			
0102419A	Aerostat Joint Project Office	190,422	190,422			
Selected Army R&D missile defense		**591,283**	**171,422**			
	Patriot Missile (PAC-3) procurement	646,590	996,590			
Total, Selected Army Missile Defense		**1,237,873**	**868,012**			
Grand Total, Missile Defense		**8,988,664**	**9,931,429**			

Table A-3. Congressional Action on Selected FY2013 Army Ground Combat Programs: Authorization

(amounts in millions of dollars)

	FY2013 Request			House-passed Authorization			Senate-passed Authorization			Authorization Conference report			
	Procurement		R&D	Procurement		R&D	Procurement		R&D	Procurement		R&D	
	#	$	$	#	$	$	#	$	$	#	$	$	
M-2 Bradley Mods		148,193	97,279		288,193	97,279		148,193	97,279				Request assumed shutdown from 2014 to 2016 of Pennsylvania plant that upgrades early-model Bradleys with improved electronics and engines. House would continue the upgrade program.
M-1 Abrams tank Mods		129,090			129,090			129,090					
M-1 Abrams tank Upgrade		74,433	82,586		255,433	82,586		165,433	82,586				Request assumed shutdown from 2014 to 2016 of Ohio plant that upgrades early-model M-1s with improved electronics, armor and engines. House would continue the upgrade program.
Stryker Armored Vehicle	58	286,818	14,347	58	286,818	14,347	58	286,818	14,347				
Ground Combat Vehicle			639,874			639,874			639,874				
Armored Multi-Purpose Vehicle			74,095			74,095			74,095				
Joint Light Tactical Vehicle			116,795			116,795			116,795				
Paladin howitzer Upgrade	17	206,101	167,797	17	206,101	167,797	17	206,101	167,797				
Hercules recovery vehicle	31	107,909		51	169,909			230,909					

Table A-4. Congressional Action on Selected FY2013 Army Ground Combat Programs: Appropriation

(amounts in millions of dollars)

	FY2013 Request			House-passed Appropriation			Senate-passed Appropriation			Appropriation Conference report			
	Procurement		R&D	Procurement		R&D	Procurement		R&D	Procurement		R&D	
	#	$	$	#	$	$	#	$	$	#	$	$	
M-2 Bradley Mods		148,193	97,279		288,193	97,279							Request assumed shutdown from 2014 to 2016 of Pennsylvania plant that upgrades early-model Bradleys with improved electronics and engines. House would continue the upgrade program.
M-1 Abrams tank Mods		129,090			129,090								
M-1 Abrams tank Upgrade		74,433	82,586		255,433	82,586							Request assumed shutdown from 2014 to 2016 of Ohio plant that upgrades early-model M-1s with improved electronics, armor and engines. House would continue the upgrade program.
Stryker Armored Vehicle	58	286,818	14,347	58	286,818	14,347							
Ground Combat Vehicle			639,874			639,874							
Armored Multi-Purpose Vehicle			74,095			74,095							
Joint Light Tactical Vehicle			116,795			116,795							
Paladin howitzer Upgrade	17	206,101	167,797	17	206,101	167,797							
Hercules recovery vehicle	31	107,909		49	169,909								

Table A-5. Congressional Action on Selected FY2013 Shipbuilding and Modernization Programs: Authorization

(amounts in millions of dollars)

	FY2013 Request			House-passed Authorization			Senate-passed Authorization			Authorization Conference report			
	Procurement		R&D	Procurement		R&D	Procurement		R&D	Procurement		R&D	
	#	$	$	#	$	$	#	$	$	#	$	$	
CVN-21 Carrier	1	608,195	159,554	1	608,195	159,554	1	608,195	159,554				The projected $11.4 billion total procurement cost of this carrier, *John F. Kennedy* (CVN-79), scheduled for delivery in 2022, is to be spread across 12 budgets (FY2007-18).
Carrier Refueling Overhaul	1	1,683,402		1	1,683,402		1	1,683,402					The projected $4.5 billion total cost of refueling and modernizing the carrier *Abraham Lincoln* (CVN-72) scheduled for completion in 2016, is to be spread across six budgets (FY2009-14)
Virginia-class submarine	2	4,092,479	165,230	2	4,870,479	165,230	2	4,870,158	165,230				Request includes $3.2 billion for two subs and $875 million for long lead-time components for one sub to be funded in FY2014 and two to be funded in FY2015. House bill adds $778 million to buy long lead-time components for a second FY2014 sub
SSBN(X)			564,912			939,312			564,912				Request includes $483.1 million to design a replacement missile-launching sub and $81.8 million to develop its nuclear powerplant. House bill increases the ship design funding by $374.4 million.
DDG-1000 Destroyer		669,222	204,202		669,222	204,202		669,222	204,202				Provides components for three ships funded largely in FY2007 and FY2009 budgets, slated for delivery in FY2014 through FY2018 at a total cost of $11.9 billion.
DDG-51 Destroyer	2	3,514,941	13,710	2	3,629,941	13,710	2	3,514,941	13,710				Request includes $3.0 billion for two ships and $466 million for long lead-time components for future ships acquired under a multi-year (FY2013-FY2017) contract for nine ships. House bill adds funds for a 10th ship.

	FY2013 Request	House-passed Authorization	Senate-passed Authorization	Authorization Conference report	
Cruiser modernization	101,000 260,616	184,972 511,741	101,000 260,616		In February 2011, DOD projected requesting $601 million in FY2013 for this multi-year program to modernize the 22 Aegis cruisers currently in service. The actual FY2013 request reflects the Administration's decision to retire the seven oldest cruisers—four in FY2013 and three in FY2014. To keep in service three of the four ships slated for retirement in FY2013, the House adds $83.9 million to this line, $170 million for new helicopters, and $26.7 million to various other modernization-related procurement programs and $84.0 million in R&D.
Destroyer modernization	452,371 233,596	452,371 233,596	452,371 233,596		Funds one year increment of a $5.4 billion multi-year program to modernize the Aegis combat system and other components of the 28 oldest DDG-51 class destroyers
Improved Anti-aircraft/Anti-Missile radar	223,621	223,621	223,621		Funds development of Advanced Missile Defense Radar (AMDR) slated to equip modified DDG-51s funded starting in FY2016. FY2013 request is $93.6 million less than had been projected in February 2011.
Littoral Combat Ship (LCS)	4 1,784,959 429,420	4 1,784,959 429,420	4 1,784,959 429,420		
LCS Combat Modules	102,608 195,824	102,608 195,824	102,608 195,824		Request funds procurement of modularized equipment sets with which an LCS can carry out minesweeping, counter-small boat or anti-submarine missions.
Joint High-Speed Vessel	1 189,196 1,967	1 189,196 1,967	189,196 1,967		

Table A-6. Congressional Action on Selected FY2013 Shipbuilding and Modernization Programs: Appropriation

(amounts in millions of dollars)

	FY2013 Request			House-passed Appropriation			Senate-passed Appropriation			Appropriation Conference report			
	#	Procurement $	R&D $	#	Procurement $	R&D $	#	Procurement $	R&D $	#	Procurement $	R&D $	
CVN-21 Carrier	1	608,195	159,554	1	578,295	159,554							The projected $11.4 billion total procurement cost of this carrier, *John F. Kennedy* (CVN-79), scheduled for delivery in 2022, is to be spread across 12 budgets (FY2007-FY2018).
Carrier Refueling Overhaul	1	1,613,402		1	1,613,402								The projected $4.5 billion total cost of refueling and modernizing the carrier *Abraham Lincoln* (CVN-72) scheduled for completion in 2016, is to be spread across six budgets (FY2009-FY2014)
Virginia-class submarine	2	4,092,479	165,230	2	4,870,479	165,230							Request includes $3.2 billion for two subs and $875 million for long lead-time components for one sub to be funded in FY2014 and two to be funded in FY2015. House bill adds $723 million to buy long lead-time components for a second FY2014 sub
SSBN(X)			564,912			939,312							Request includes $483.1 million to design a replacement missile-launching sub and $81.8 million to develop its nuclear powerplant.
DDG-1000 Destroyer		669,222	204,202		669,222	204,202							Provides components for three ships funded largely in FY2007 and FY2009 budgets, slated for delivery in FY2014 through FY2018 at a total cost of $11.9 billion.
DDG-51 Destroyer	2	3,514,941	13,710	3	4,502,911	13,710							Request includes $3.0 billion for two ships and $466 million for long lead-time components for future ships acquired under a multi-year (FY2013-FY2017) contract for nine ships. House bill adds $1.0 billion for a 10th ship.

	FY2013 Request		House-passed Appropriation		Senate-passed Appropriation	Appropriation Conference report
Cruiser modernization	101,000	260,616	607,660	510,616		In February 2011, DOD projected requesting $601 million in FY2013 for this multi-year program to modernize the 22 Aegis cruisers currently in service. The actual FY2013 request reflects the Administration's decision to retire the seven oldest cruisers—four in FY2013 and three in FY2014. As part of its decision to keep in service three of the four ships, the House added $256.7 million. It also added an additional $250.0 million to equip for anti-missile defense several ships not currently slated to receive that capability.
Destroyer modernization	452,371	233,596	412,656	233,596		Funds one year increment of a $5.4 billion multi-year program to modernize the Aegis combat system and other components of the 28 oldest DDG-51 class destroyers
Improved Anti-aircraft/Anti-Missile radar		223,621		223,621		Funds development of Advanced Missile Defense Radar (AMDR) slated to equip modified DDG-51s funded starting in FY2016. FY2013 request is $93.6 million less than had been projected in February 2011.
Littoral Combat Ship (LCS)	4 1,784,959	429,420	4 1,784,959	401,620		
LCS Combat Modules	102,608	195,824	102,608	195,824		Request funds procurement of modularized equipment sets with which an LCS can carry out minesweeping, counter-small boat or anti-submarine missions.
Joint High-Speed Vessel	1 189,196	1,967	189,196	1,967		

Table A-7. Congressional Action on Selected FY2013 Space Programs: Authorization

(amounts in millions of dollars)

	FY2013 Request			House-passed Authorization			Senate-passed Authorization			Authorization Conference report			
	Procurement	R&D		Procurement	R&D		Procurement	R&D		Procurement	R&D		
	#	$	$	#	$	$	#	$	$	#	$	$	
Advanced EHF Satellite		557,205	229,171		557,205	227,671		557,205	227,671				Request funds purchase of fifth and sixth of a new type of communications satellite with greater capacity and jam-resistance than earlier types
GPS III Satellite	2	492,910	690,587	2	492,910	689,087	2	492,910	689,087				Request funds improved navigation satellites to sustain a 24 satellite constellation
Evolved Expendable Launch Vehicle (EELV)	4	1,679,856	7.980	4	1,679,856	7.980	4	1,679,856	7.980				
SBIR High	2	454,251	448,594	2	454,251	446,594	2	454,251	447,094				Request funds purchase of the fifth and sixth of a new type of infra-red sensor satellites to detect ballistic missile launches
"Space Fence"		0.0	252,578		0.0	232,578		0.0	252,578				Continues development of "Space Fence" to monitor orbital debris that could endanger U.S. satellites

Table A-8. Congressional Action on Selected FY2013 Space Programs: Appropriation

(amounts in millions of dollars)

	FY2013 Request			House-passed Appropriation			Senate-passed Appropriation			Appropriation Conference report			
	#	Procurement $	R&D $	#	Procurement $	R&D $	#	Procurement $	R&D $	#	Procurement $	R&D $	
Advanced EHF Satellite		557,205	229,171		547,205	191.171							Request funds purchase of fifth and sixth of a new type of communications satellite with greater capacity and jam-resistance than earlier types
GPS III Satellite	2	492,910	690,587	2	492,910	652,287							Request funds improved navigation satellites to sustain a 24 satellite constellation
Evolved Expendable Launch Vehicle (EELV)	4	1,679,856	7,980	4	1,679,856	32,980							
SBIR High	2	454,251	448,594	2	454,251	516,594							Request funds purchase of the fifth and sixth of a new type of infra-red sensor satellites to detect ballistic missile launches
"Space Fence"	0	0.0	252,578	0	0.0	215,478							Continues development of "Space Fence" to monitor orbital debris that could endanger U.S. satellites

Table A-9. Congressional Action on Selected FY2013 Aircraft and Long-Range Missile Programs: Authorization

(amounts in millions of dollars)

	FY2013 Request			House-passed Authorization			Senate-passed Authorization			Authorization Conference report			
	Procurement		R&D	Procurement		R&D	Procurement		R&D	Procurement		R&D	
	#	$	$	#	$	$	#	$	$	#	$	$	
Fixed Wing Tactical Combat Aircraft													
F-35A Joint Strike Fighter and Mods, AF (conventional takeoff version)	19	3,417,702	1,210,306	19	3,353,702	1,210,306	19	3,417,702	1,210,306				
F-35B Joint Strike Fighter, Marine Corps (STOVL version)	6	1,510,936	737,149	6	1,510,936	733,949	6	1,510,936	737,149				
F-35C Joint Strike Fighter, Navy (Carrier-based version)	4	1,072,812	743,926	4	1,072,812	740,726	4	1,072,812	743,926				
[F-35 Joint Strike Fighter, total]													
F-35 Fighter Mods		147,995	8,117		147,995	8,117		147,995	8,117				
F-22 Fighter Mods		283,871	511,767		283,871	511,767		283,871	511,767				
F-15 Fighter Mods		148,378	192,677		148,378	192,677		148,378	192,677				
F-16 Fighter Mods		6,896	190,257		6,896	190,257		6,896	190,257				
EA-18G Electronic Warfare Acft.	12	1,027,443	13,009	12	1,042,443	13,009	12	1,027,443	13,009				
F/A-18E/F Fighter	26	2,065,427		26	2,019,427		26	2,125,427					Request includes no funds for long-lead components to continue procurement in FY2014; House adds $45 million for long-lead components to allow future production partly offset by reductions of $30.0 million.

	FY2013 Request	House-passed Authorization	Senate-passed Authorization	Authorization Conference report
F/A-18 Fighter Mods	688,549	188,299	188,299	
A-10 Attack Plane Mods	89,919	13,358	13,358	
Long-Range Strike Aircraft and Missiles				
Long-Range Strike (Aircraft)	0.0	291,742	291,742	
B-1B Bomber Mods	149,756	16,265	16,265	
B-2A Bomber Mods	82,296	317,026	302,026	S. 3254 would cut $15.0 million from R&D request for unspecified "efficiencies."
B-52 Bomber Mods	9,781	53,208	53,208	
Trident II Missile Mods	1,224,683	101,295	101,295	Request funds service-life extension of multi-warhead, nuclear-armed, sub-launched ballistic missiles
Conventional Prompt Global Strike	0.0	110,383	110,383	
Fixed-Wing and Tilt-Rotor Cargo and Transport Aircraft				
C-130 variants, including Mods	7 1,167,145	7 50,299	50,299	
C-5 Mods,	1,127,586	35,115	35,115	
C-17 Mods	205,079	99,225	99,225	
C-27 Joint Cargo Aircraft	0.0	115,000	0.0	
V-22 Osprey, including Mods	21 2,025,426	84,261	84,261	
Fixed-Wing Surveillance and Tanker Aircraft				
KC-46 Tanker	0.0 1,815,588	1,815,588	1,728,458	

Rotary-Wing Aircraft (including SOF) and other aircraft — FY2013 authorization ($ in thousands)

Item	FY2013 Request		House-passed Authorization		Senate-passed Authorization		Authorization Conference report	
	Qty	$	Qty	$	Qty	$	$	Notes
E-8C Joint Stars		59,320		59,320		71,320	24,241	
P-8A Poseidon	13	2,746,434	13	2,746,434	13	2,746,434	421,102	
P-3/EP-3 Mods		227,809		227,809		227,809	3,405	
E-2D Hawkeye	5	984,677	5	984,677	5	984,677	119,065	
E-3A AWACS Mods		193,099		193,099		193,099	65,200	
Rotary-Wing Aircraft (including SOF)								
UH-60 Blackhawk	59	1,222,200	59	1,222,200	59	1,222,200	83,255*	
Blackhawk Mods		200,584		200,584		200,584		
AH-64 Apache Block III	50	1,055,936	50	1,055,936	48	984,936	124,450*	Request would remanufacture 40 helos and buy 10 new ones, all with improved electronics and weaponry
Apache Mods		178,805		178,805		178,805		
CH-47 Chinook	44	1,390,682	44	1,390,682	44	1,390,682	71,563*	Request would remanufacture 19 helos and buy 25 new ones, all with improved electronics and engines
Chinook Mods		173,920		173,920		173,920		
Light Utility Helicopter	34	271,983	34	271,983	34	271,983		
OH-58 Kiowa Upgrade		376,384		376,384		376,384	85,468	
Huey/SuperCobra Upgrades	28	820,391	28	820,391	28	820,391	31,105	
MH-60R/S Seahawk	37	1,296,831	42	1,466,831	37	1,296,831	36,609	
CH-53K	0.0	606,204		0.0		0.0	606,204	
Unmanned Aerial Systems (including Mods)								
Predator and Reaper		1,673,727		1,891,027		1,732,127	231,711	

Program	FY2013 Request	House-passed Authorization	Senate-passed Authorization	Authorization Conference report
Global Hawk	95,911 1,103,857	201,111 1,103,857	95,911 1,103,857	1,103,857
Unmanned Combat Air Vehicle (UCAV)	142,282	217,282	142,282	142,282
Unmanned Carrier-Launched Airborne Surveillance and Strike (UCLASS)	122,481	47,481	122,481	122,481
Fire Scout	6 141,073 99,600	6 141,073 99,600	141,073 99,600	6 99,600
Shadow	153,663 39,621	153,663 39,621	153,663 39,621	39,621
Raven	30,178 4,534	30,178 4,534	30,178 4,534	4,534

Table A-10. Congressional Action on Selected FY2013 Aircraft and Long-Range Missile Programs: Appropriation

(amounts in millions of dollars)

	FY2013 Request			House-passed Appropriation			Senate-passed Appropriation			Appropriation Conference report		
	Procurement		R&D	Procurement		R&D	Procurement		R&D	Procurement		R&D
	#	$	$	#	$	$	#	$	$	#	$	$
Fixed Wing Tactical Combat Aircraft												
F-35A Joint Strike Fighter and Mods, AF (conventional takeoff version)	19	3,417,702	1,210,306	19	3,244,702	1,210,306						
F-35B Joint Strike Fighter, Marine Corps (STOVL version)	6	1,510,936	737,149	6	1,343,835	733,949						
F-35C Joint Strike Fighter, Navy (Carrier-based version)	4	1,072,812	743,926	4	998,569	740,726						
[F-35 Joint Strike Fighter, total]												
F-35 Fighter Mods		147,995	8,117		30,195	0.0						
F-22 Fighter Mods		283,871	511,767		333,871	511,767						
F-15 Fighter Mods		148,378	192,677		148,378	192,677						
F-16 Fighter Mods		6,896	190,257		6,896	190,257						
EA-18G Electronic Warfare Acft.	12	1,027,443	13,009	12	985,965	13,009						
F/A-18E/F Fighter	26	2,065,427		37	2,627,861							
F/A-18 Fighter Mods		688,549	188,299		641,262	168,299						
A-10 Attack Plane Mods		89,919	13,358		89,919	13,358						

	FY2013 Request	House-passed Appropriation	Senate-passed Appropriation	Appropriation Conference report
Long-Range Strike Aircraft and Missiles				
Long-Range Strike (Aircraft)	0.0	291,742		
B-1B Bomber Mods	149,756	16,265		
B-2A Bomber Mods	82,296	317,026		
B-52 Bomber Mods	53,208 / 9,781	18,508		
Trident II Missile Mods	1,224,683	101,295		Request funds service-life extension of multi-warhead, nuclear-armed, sub-launched ballistic missiles
Conventional Prompt Global Strike	110,383	110,383		
Fixed-Wing and Tilt-Rotor Cargo and Transport Aircraft				
C-130 variants, including Mods	7 / 1,167,145 / 50,299	14 / 1,624,145 / 50,299		
C-5 Mods,	1,127,586 / 35,115	1,053,586 / 35,115		
C-17 Mods	205,079 / 99,225	205,079 / 35,115		
C-27 Joint Cargo Aircraft	0.0	115,000 / 25,000		
V-22 Osprey, including Mods.	21 / 2,025,426 / 84,261	22 / 2,066,451 / 73,261		
Fixed-Wing Surveillance and Tanker Aircraft				
KC-46 Tanker	0.0 / 1,815,588	0.0 / 1,815,588		
E-8C Joint Stars	59,320 / 24,241	49,020 / 24,241		
P-8A Poseidon	13 / 2,746,434 / 421,102	13 / 2,712,731 / 406,102		
P-3/EP-3 Mods	227,809 / 3,405	218,309 / 3,405		
E-2D Hawkeye	5 / 984,677 / 119,065	5 / 937,677 / 119,065		

Program	FY2013 Request	House-passed Appropriation	Senate-passed Appropriation	Appropriation Conference report
E-3A AWACS Mods	193,099 / 65,200	193,099 / 48,900		
Rotary-Wing Aircraft (including SOF)				
UH-60 Blackhawk	59 / 1,222,200 / 83,255	69 / 1,461,100 / 83,255*		
Blackhawk Mods	200,584	220,584		
AH-64 Apache Block III	50 / 1,055,936 / 124,450	50 / 1,090,936 / 124,450*		Request would remanufacture 40 helos and buy 10 new ones, all with improved electronics and weaponry
Apache Mods	178,805	178,805		
CH-47 Chinook	44 / 1,390,682 / 71,563	44 / 1,390,682 / 71,563*		Request would remanufacture 19 helos and buy 25 new ones, all with improved electronics and engines
Chinook Mods	173,920	192,420		
Light Utility Helicopter	34 / 271,983	37 / 295,980		
OH-58 Kiowa Upgrade	376,384 / 85,468	376,384 / 85,468		
Huey/SuperCobra Upgrades	28 / 820,391 / 31,105	30 / 856,773 / 31,105		
MH-60R/S Seahawk	37 / 1,296,831 / 36,609	42 / 1,433,852 / 36,609		
CH-53K	0.0 / 606,204	0.0 / 606,204		
Unmanned Aerial Systems (including Mods)				
Predator and Reaper	43 / 1,673,727 / 231,711	55 / 1,863,727 / 231,711		
Global Hawk	95,911 / 1,103,857	202,911 / 1,119,857		
Unmanned Combat Air Vehicle (UCAV)	142,282	142,282		

	FY2013 Request		House-passed Appropriation		Senate-passed Appropriation	Appropriation Conference report
Unmanned Carrier-Launched Airborne Surveillance and Strike (UCLASS)		122,481		122,481		
Fire Scout	6	141,073	6	70,073	83,100	
		99,600				
Shadow		153,663		153,663	39,621	
		39,621				
Raven		30,178		30,178	4,534	
		4,534				

Author Contact Information

Pat Towell
Specialist in U.S.
Defense Policy and
Budget
ptowell@crs.loc.gov, 7-
2122

Daniel H. Else
Specialist in National
Defense
delse@crs.loc.gov, 7-
4996

Key Policy Staff

Area of Expertise	Name	Phone	E-mail
War costs	Amy Belasco	7-7627	abelasco@crs.loc.gov
Intelligence	Richard Grimmett	7-7675	rgrimmett@crs.loc.gov
Military personnel social issues	David Burrelli	7-8033	dburrelli@crs.loc.gov
Force Structure and policy	Catherine Dale	7-8983	cdale@crs.loc.gov
Acquisition workforce	Valerie Grasso	7-7617	vgrasso@crs.loc.gov
Military compensation	Lawrence Kapp	7-7609	lkapp@crs.loc.gov
Health care	Don Jansen	4-4769	djansen@crs.loc.gov
Reserve component issues	Lawrence Kapp	7-7609	lkapp@crs.loc.gov
Acquisition process	Moshe Schwartz	7-1463	mschwartz@crs.loc.gov
Military construction and installations, defense industry	Daniel H. Else	7-4996	delse@crs.loc.gov
Current military operations	Catherine Dale	7-8983	cdale@crs.loc.gov
Ground combat systems	Andrew Feickert	7-7673	afeickert@crs.loc.gov
Military aviation systems	Jeremiah Gertler	7-5107	jgertler@crs.loc.gov
Missile defense systems	Steven Hildreth	7-7635	shildreth@crs.loc.gov
Nuclear weapons	Jonathan Medalia	7-7632	jmedalia@crs.loc.gov
Naval systems	Ronald O'Rourke	7-7610	rorourke@crs.loc.gov
Cyber-warfare	Catherine Theohary	7-0844	ctheohary@crs.loc.gov